**Neera Chandhoke** is Distinguished Fellow at the Centre for Equity Studies, New Delhi. She was formerly Professor of Political Science and the Director of the Developing Countries Research Centre at the University of Delhi. She has held several fellowships abroad and has authored many research papers and books. Some of her recent books include *Violence in Our Bones* (2021), *Rethinking Pluralism, Secularism, Tolerance: Anxieties of Co-Existence* (2019), *Democracy and Revolutionary Politics* (2015) and *Contested Secessions* (2012). She is a frequent contributor to print and online publications such as *The Hindu*, *The Wire*, *The Indian Express* and *The Tribune*.

# We, the People, and Our Constitution

Neera Chandhoke

SPEAKING
TIGER

SPEAKING TIGER BOOKS LLP
125A, Ground Floor, Shahpur Jat, near Asiad Village,
New Delhi 110049

First published by Speaking Tiger Books 2024



ISBN: 978-93-5447-668-6
eISBN: 978-93-5447-669-3

10 9 8 7 6 5 4 3 2 1



Typeset in Garamond Premier Pro by SÜRYA, New Delhi
Printed at ...

# CONTENTS

# A People's Logbook of Pledges and Dreams

*Harsh Mander*

Having shaken off the shackles of two hundred years of slavery in 1947, the Indian people chose to draw up the blueprint of the kind of country free India would be. Unlike several other countries that had newly gained independence around the time, India did adopt wholly or partly a constitution left behind by the departing colonizer. The Indian people resolved proudly that they would write their own destiny, and they did so with solemn and searching reflection and debate for several years.

At the time of India's freedom, the world was still rebuilding and healing from the devastation and wounds left by the Second World War. The Holocaust had left around six million Jews, two-thirds of the entire Jewish people in Europe, dead, many in gas chambers built in Nazi Germany, the state led by Adolf Hitler from 1933 to 1945; along with multitudes of Roma and Sinti people, homosexual men, persons with disability and prisoners of war. The people of the world were learning from this horrific and tragic genocide the dangers of what happens in a country if minorities—religious, racial, ethnic, caste, sexual—are not protected. They were learning the cataclysmic consequences of the politics of hate and division. These were also lessons for the Indian people. The same lessons came out of the horrific Partition riots, and from India's epic freedom struggle.

## India's Struggle for Freedom

Mahatma Gandhi returned to India from the distant shores of South Africa in 1915. He was forty-five years old. The India he returned to, not unlike the one he had left as a young man, was mired in many unfreedoms, the primary one for a great many being political, enslaved as India was to rulers from across the seas for nearly two lightless centuries.

The colonial government could throw for years into prison people who rallied or fought against their rule. Some were hung from the gallows like the heroic young revolutionary, Bhagat Singh, some were banished for lifetimes to the distant Andaman Islands. Even those committed to peaceful, non-violent resistance to foreign rule were beaten back and often bundled into jail, sometimes for long periods of time.

The British colonized India because, at the time they arrived, this was one of the wealthiest and most industrialized countries in the world. In the two centuries of their rule, most industries had been destroyed, farming starved through rack-renting and artisans impoverished. There was misery and hunger in the famine-ravished countryside. The average lifespan of a common Indian was as low as 21 years at the time when Gandhiji returned to India.

The Indian people endured the agony of painful bondage in ways similar to the people of many countries in Asia, Africa and Latin America. A handful of Western countries had carved out large chunks of the globe, rich in natural resources. They devised various systems for arrogating the resources of these countries to their own ends: cotton for their mills, tea for their trade, land for their *lagaan*, food for their granaries, markets for their produce and soldiers for their wars.

The proud people of these enslaved countries, including India, rose heroically in revolt. All struggling people found their own pathways to freedom. What marks out our freedom struggle from most others was that the mainstream of our struggle was founded on the pivotal moral idea of *ahimsa*, or non-violence. Ahimsa means the resolve that I will fight you for my freedom and dignity, resolutely, accepting whatever consequences this battle will extract from me, including a bullet or banishment to prison; but even as I struggle against you for what is right and just, I will never hate you, and I will wish or cause you no injury or harm.

### A Broken, Wounded India

The British eventually bent to the resilience of this struggle. However, they left not one but two nations—India and Pakistan. In frenzied riots on both sides of the new border which now suddenly separated sister from sister and brother from brother, a madness of hate seized the sub-continent. Hindus, Muslims and Sikhs slaughtered each other with a viciousness that cast a very dark and long shadow on the celebrations of freedom. Estimates of mortality range up to two million; an uncounted number were raped and abducted. Fourteen million people were cruelly uprooted from their homes, travelling often on foot, weary and heartbroken, for hundreds of kilometres, with their small children and the few belongings that they had been able to salvage on their aching backs. There is only one other distress migration, which humankind has witnessed in the course of recorded history, that was larger than this one. This was the forced trafficking of Africans as slaves to the Americas.

Pakistan was created as an independent nation for the Muslim people who lived in the west and east flanks of the teeming country. Its leaders urged Muslims in other parts of India to move to Pakistan to make this new nation their home.

There were some who advocated that India should be a country *only* for the Hindus—a Hindu India, a mirror image of a Muslim Pakistan. This would be a fitting reply to Pakistan, they felt, and would secure justice to India's overwhelming Hindu majority.

But Gandhiji had led our freedom struggle on the shining promise that India would be a country where people of every religion (or no religion!), caste, language and gender would be equal citizens in every way. Jawaharlal Nehru, India's first prime minister, declared that India would belong equally to all those who chose to make this their home, irrespective of their religion or community. One of Gandhi's closest associates, Maulana Azad, often spoke glowingly of his great pride, sense of ownership and resolute belonging to this country which he so loved. He declared that he was Muslim *and* he was Indian, and both these identities were inseparable from him, that he was willing to give up neither of these. He said India had given a great deal to its Muslim people, and the Muslim people too had given a great deal to their country. On 23 October 1947, as the country was reeling under the Partition, he stood tall on the ramparts of the grand Jama Masjid in Delhi and made a historic, heartfelt appeal to Muslims living in various parts of India to stay on, because this was their country and would always be.

This call was echoed over and over again by a Gandhi devastated to his soul by the tumult of religious hate and violence in India and Pakistan. He entreated Muslims over and over again to stay on in an India that he pledged would belong equally, in every way, to its Muslim citizens. A very large number of Muslims heeded his call, and the call of Maulana Azad and Jawaharlal Nehru, opting for multi-faith India over Muslim Pakistan.

When India was celebrating freedom in August 1947, however, Mahatma Gandhi was not in Delhi to celebrate as the Union Jack was lowered and the Indian Tricolour raised. He was instead in Calcutta, where Muslims and Hindus were killing each other in what appeared to be an unending bloodbath of hate. He went on an epic fast refusing to eat a morsel of food until the last of the violence had ended. He returned then to Delhi, trying to quell the hate and violence of hundreds of thousands of angry and sullen refugees separated forever from their homeland in what was now Pakistan. (These included my own extended family, uprooted from their birthplace.) He had planned then to travel (pointedly without a visa) into Pakistan to try to douse the fires of hatred that raged in this newly born country. But this was not to be.

Every day, Mahatma Gandhi would hold a prayer meeting, in which he recited prayers from all major religions. One of his favourite hymns included the line: '*Ishwar-Allah tero naam*'. On a winter evening on 30 January 1948, on his way to his prayer meeting, he was killed by a man violently opposed to his idea of an India which would belong equally to all people of all faiths. A stricken people mourned the death of the father of the nation, a man who paved the path to building a country which was humane and inclusive, which assured equal rights as citizens to people of every religion, caste, language and gender.

Babasaheb Ambedkar, who would lead the writing of India's constitution, had warned that any attempt to restrict India to people of the majority Hindu faith would be a 'calamity' for the nation and for democracy.

As the bullets of Gandhi's assassin signalled, not everyone shared this vision for India.

## The Constitution—a Dream, a Vision, a Set of Promises

Centuries of colonial bondage had reduced India from one of the wealthiest to one of the poorest countries of the world, in which famine, illiteracy, sickness and want stalked the countryside. For millennia, the cruel system of caste had made life a living hell for those unfortunate enough to be born into disadvantaged castes. Women were denied rights to property, education, work and dignity, and even sometimes life itself.

Would we change all of this, and how? Who would this

country belong to? Who would govern this country? How would the rulers be chosen? What powers would these rulers have? What powers and rights would the people have? And would the country's minorities—religious, caste, tribal and gender—be protected?

It was answers to questions like these that were written into the Constitution of newly independent India.

What is a constitution? It is a dream, a vision, a set of promises; a compendium of guarantees, a store-house of aspirations. It is a solemn articulation of the values that the country will hold close to its collective soul in its journey in the decades and centuries which lie ahead. It is the collective imagination of the destination which the country pledges to reach.

Most constitutions, except for those in the United Kingdom, Israel, Saudi Arabia and a few others, are written documents. The Constitution of India was written by a collective, the Constituent Assembly. They sat in the grand historic circular building which became for over seven decades the Parliament of the Indian republic. The Constituent Assembly had over three hundred members. These women and men were, in a sense, the founding mothers and fathers of the Constitution. They were drawn from the people elected into the provincial assemblies of the time. And about a third were nominated, to ensure that those in attendance included people of every religion, caste, gender, culture, community and profession. The Constituent Assembly did not have members only from the Congress party which led India to freedom; members were invited even from parties strongly opposed to the Congress.

One example is Babasaheb Bhimrao Ambedkar, who was the brave, charismatic and inspiring leader of the Scheduled Castes Federation, who had often stood in stout opposition to the Congress led by Gandhiji. Members of the Hindu Right were also invited to sit in the Constituent Assembly. There were many small kingdoms which were merged into the Indian nation, and their representatives were also members of this assembly.

Looking back today, we realize that it should have had many more women, more persons with disability, more Adivasi and Dalit people, many more working poor people, from factories and farms, and more gender minorities. But there's no denying the fact that the fine women and men who sat on the benches of the Constituent Assembly did indeed speak for all the people of India.

The first sittings of the Constituent Assembly began even before India became free, in the winter of 1946. The assembly deliberated for three years. A smaller group was carved out of the assembly called the Drafting Committee, which worked on the detailed draft of the constitution, and each of the sections of this draft were discussed in the assembly and then put to vote.

The chairperson of this drafting committee was one of the most learned men in the assembly, Dr Ambedkar, affectionately called Babasaheb. He contributed invaluably to many of the progressive measures written into our constitution. He was born into a very poor family of a soldier in the Indian army, from one of the most oppressed castes. On people from these castes for centuries was inflicted the most cruel form of discrimination which we know as untouchability. (Shamefully, that and many such practices endure in free India.) The country is fortunate that such a man—highly educated, wise and one who knew from personal experience the suffering of the most oppressed of our people—led the process of writing the constitution. The two women members of the Drafting Committee, Hansa Mehta and Rajkumari Amrit Kaur, contributed spiritedly and thoughtfully to the deliberations, seeking to make the Constitution also reflect the aspirations of the forgotten and oppressed half of the population, women. We owe a lot to the founding mothers and fathers of the constitution, who drew with us and for us the contours of the dream and the promise of a country based on equality and humanity which we resolved to build, one day.

From Mahatma Gandhi, we imbibed the idea and practice of radical love. From Babasaheb Ambedkar we learned the idea and practice of radical equality. These together became the cornerstones of our Constitution.

## Hum Log: We, the People of India

Who indeed gave to us our constitution? The opening lines of the document answer this question. They tell us that 'We, the people of India' ('*Hum, Bharat ke log*') gave to ourselves this constitution. Who are 'we, the people of India'? We are the people who lived in this great and ancient land in past centuries; we are the people who were alive in India when the Constitution was framed; and we are the people of generations which followed and are still to follow. 'We' includes our grandparents and parents, it includes each of us who reside in this vast terrain today. And 'we' will include our children and their children one day.

The 'we' in 'we, the people' is the ocean in which many, many different little streams and mighty rivers meet. We derive strength and vitality from the plurality of our magnificent heritage. This kaleidoscope of our diversity is mirrored in our ever-changing natural features—from the Himalayas to the rivers, the forests to the deserts, the deltas to the plateaus, the coastlines to the islands. This kaleidoscope is made up of our music, of our art, of our dance forms, of our *gharanas* of classical music, and of their vibrant intermingling fusions. Of the spectacular range of our culinary choices, our varied taste buds that create a plethora of platters and cuisines, changing every few hundred miles. Of every festival of every religion and culture, which in our land becomes an Indian festival. Of our thousands of dialects and languages, such that if two people are selected at random from any ten in our country, chances are that they will speak different tongues.

India is the glorious symphony of our many different voices. It is a wondrous palette in which you can find every colour in the world, and we are privileged to be able to draw paintings of our lives from this multitude of colours.

All of these, all and every one of us, you and I, make 'we, the people'.

## The Preamble

The soul of the Constitution, its essence, is contained in a single page, which is called the Preamble. Every religion has a holy book, and prayer. Some people say that for the people of India, our holy book is our constitution, and our prayer the preamble.

But holy books are often placed on an unreachable pedestal; holy books cannot be questioned or changed. The Constitution is not that kind of holy book. It is a book which belongs to we, the people of India, one that protects and guides us through difficult times, but one that can be discussed, challenged and also collectively changed. It is a book of the people, not of the gods. It contains within it the values that the people of India pledge to uphold as the nation is built and as later generations come and go.

### *A Sovereign Democratic Republic*

The preamble first talks of the kind of country India will be. India will be sovereign. This means its destiny will no longer be controlled by any foreign power. It will be democratic. This means its government will be chosen by its people. It will be a republic, which means that the ruler will not be born into power, in the way kings and queens have been born for centuries. Nor will the ruler snatch power through the bloodshed and brute force of military conquest or coups. The ruler will have to be elected by the people. Anyone, including those born into the greatest disadvantage, will have the right to aspire to become rulers, and seek the support of the people for the right to rule them.

An important question arose before the Constituent Assembly about which people should have the right to vote for their government. India became the first of the newly independent countries to give *every* person—man, woman or transgender, rich or poor, educated or uneducated—exactly equal political power to choose their rulers. One person, one vote. The richest and the most powerful man in the country would have the same single vote as the poorest, most destitute trans woman. A young person born in India today may think this is the most normal thing to do, but it wasn't at the time. It was a brave and radical—and some would say audacious—idea. In Western democracies, for a long time only white men of wealth enjoyed the right to vote. Women had to fight long for an equal right to vote. In the United States of America, for instance, women got the right to vote only in 1920, and African Americans only in 1965. In Australia, aboriginal Australians did not get the right to vote until 1962. In India, the idea of universal suffrage for every person was adopted without any noteworthy dissent.

Many people had feared that Indians were not ready for this radical system of voting rights for all people, called universal adult franchise. Less than one in five people were even literate at the time of Independence; among women there were less than one in ten. But our founding mothers and fathers still resolved to place their faith in the ordinary Indian, even those denied education, wealth and social standing. They ensured that they would be guaranteed as their birth-right the opportunity to participate equally with every other Indian, the most wealthy, educated, socially or politically powerful, in choosing their governments, and through this, in building the nation and their collective destinies. For a society that would not allow the 'lower' castes to step inside schools and temples, to possess land, and to live with dignity; for a society that would not allow some women even the chance to be born, let alone to own and inherit property and to work shoulder to shoulder with men—for this society to resolve to ensure the same and equal right to vote for every person, though not the end of the road, was a truly iridescent beginning to the great adventure of building a new nation.

From the first election in India in 1951, people from around the world watched with wonder and admiration as impoverished people, disadvantaged castes and women formed the longest lines outside polling booths. This has remained unchanged even until today. India's people of disadvantage are found to choose carefully and thoughtfully. The wonderment is that the people democracy has most let down are those who continue to have the greatest faith in this same democracy.

### *Socialist and Secular*

The preamble goes on to mandate that the country will be socialist. This means many things. That the government must be committed to ensuring a decent standard of living for all its citizens. It must protect them from hunger and joblessness, and ensure equal and affordable education, health care, housing, decent work and social protection to all. It means a conscious state resolve to prevent the concentration of wealth in a few hands.

The preamble also lays down that India will be a secular country. This means that the government will have no religion, and it will neither practise nor promote any particular religion. It will not discriminate in any way between people on the basis of their religion, whether they form a tiny minority of people, numbering not more than a few hundred people, following their traditional faith, or those who follow the religion of the largest majority of the Indian people. It also means that the state will promote harmony and goodwill between people with different belief systems.

In a particularly significant judgement of the Delhi High Court which decriminalized homosexuality in 2006, despite the stout opposition of people of almost every religious faith in the country, the bench declared that India's secular constitution gives every citizen of the country the freedom to follow their faith and beliefs. Of course, if their moral rules contradict the morality of the Constitution, it is constitutional morality that must prevail over individual religious beliefs. This iridescent ruling was first overturned by the Supreme Court, and then restored, but sexual minorities are still denied the equal right of people of the same sex to marry.

### Justice

The Constitution promises equal justice to all people, in all aspects of their lives. Justice here does not simply mean what goes on in the courts. It means fairness. It means that people will not face discrimination in society because of their religion, caste, gender, sexuality or disability. They will not face discrimination in their participation in the economy, in work and in the markets. Women and men (and gay and trans people) will have equal access to employment, based only on their merit and not their gender, and will get equal pay for equal work. The ancient system of *begar*, or forced labour, imposed mostly on the most disadvantaged castes was abolished by the Constitution. No one could be kept as a bonded labourer. Every person will also be treated fairly in their political life, when they go out to vote, to campaign, or to fight elections.

### *Liberty*

One of the most important promises of the constitution is of liberty, or freedom. In many protests around the country, slogans are raised for *azaadi*. Azaadi means liberty or freedom. What kinds of freedom or azaadi does the Constitution guarantee? It mandates freedom of thought, expression and belief. This means that every citizen is free to think, speak and believe in ideas which may not conform to the views of the government in power, or of the majority of people. In other words, it grants the freedom of conscience, the freedom to dissent, to disagree with power—political, social and economic power. Many believe that this freedom lies at the core of democracy.

The right to dissent must also carry the freedom from fear, the assurance that I will not be punished for holding beliefs different from those of the powerful. Rabindranath Tagore speaks glowingly of such a country, in which 'the mind is without fear, and the head is held high...' History stands witness that it was only when brave women and men raised their voices against established orthodoxies of their time—when Galileo said the world was round and not flat, or when Savitribai Phule and Fatima Sheikh established schools for girls when the kitchen was believed to be the only fitting confine for women, when Raja Ram Mohan Roy railed against a woman being burnt on her husband's pyre for *sati* or children being tied in marriage, when Babasaheb Ambedkar fought the idea and practice of caste in which the accident of your birth determines all your life chances, condemning you to a life of humiliation and discrimination, barring you from education and dignified work—that the world became a better place for later generations. We are here today because they refused to conform. Conformity leads to deadwood and regression. The freedom of conscience, the freedom to dissent, is therefore central to the pledge of liberty for all, which our constitution guarantees.

The Constitution also importantly assures the freedom of faith and worship. It protects the right of every person to follow her religion, her forms of worship, her ways of life including her choice of food and clothes. It allows people not just to follow but also to propagate their faith, and to establish their religious institutions.

There are other vital freedoms as well which are mandated by our constitution. These include the freedom to pursue the occupation we choose, to move to any part of the country and to form associations or unions, to write and produce art, poetry, novels, books, philosophy, theatre, films—and video games and Instagram videos—which reflect our belief systems and our creativity.

### *Equality*

There are many ways that we are not equal. Some of us run faster than others, some cook better, some sing or dance or paint better, some score better marks in class, some can become mothers and others cannot, and so on. But above all of these differences, the Constitution recognizes us all to be equal in a fundamental way: we are equal in human dignity and human worth. There is, from this yardstick, no difference between the wealthiest person and someone begging for alms outside a temple or dargah. It is because of this inherent intrinsic equality that we all have an equal vote and equal rights and freedoms.

The Constitution requires that the government should ensure equality of opportunity. This means that wherever you might be born, in a village, a slum, the city streets or a mansion, you are entitled to the same opportunities to study, in the same quality school or college, and the same chances to develop your potential, whether for intellectual pursuit, sports, music, art or anything else. It also requires governments to ensure equality of status. This is an even more difficult task. It means that at least to some degree, governments must ensure more equal conditions of life to those who are more disadvantaged. This can only be done by what is called redistribution, by taxing the wealthy to ensure the right to a decent life to the disadvantaged; and by reservations or affirmative action, which recognizes that people who have for centuries been treated unequally need special support in education and jobs for them to achieve real equality in the conditions of their lives.

The Constitution also firmly and categorically bans the practice of untouchability. This—along with the principle of one person, one vote—are arguably the most radical sections of the Constitution. It outlaws unambiguously a practice that has brutalized and shamed Indian society for at least two millennia. Untouchability is one of the most troubling, cruel and disgraceful parts of India's historical legacy. By the accident of birth into a particular caste, it condemns people to a life where they are not allowed into religious shrines, share food or water with other people who will avoid so much as their touch, and will prevent them from walking on the same road as them or riding a horse in a wedding procession, or studying in school or college. The Constitution prohibited these shameful practices. This provision transforms the Constitution, at least in part, into a luminous moral document, seeking to confront and atone for the crimes of our history.

### *Fraternity*

Fraternity in English means brotherhood. This must of course include sisterhood as well. The Hindi version of the Constitution uses the beautiful word *bandhuta*. Derived from Sanskrit, this means the idea that we are bound to and with each other. Looking at it in another way, *bandhu* means friend, so bandhuta can also be understood as an ideology of friendship.

Fraternity or bandhuta encompasses the lustrous idea that we might have between us enormous differences—of wealth, gender, caste, religion, language, ability, the colour of our skins, the size of our eyes and noses, who we choose to love and marry, the food we eat, the clothes we wear, and so much else—but are *bound to and with each other* despite that. We are brothers, sisters, friends.

Dr Ambedkar rightly said that the most important idea in the Constitution is the idea of fraternity. It is this idea which affirms the equal dignity of every individual. We learn from him that the other foundational ideas of the Constitution—justice, liberty, equality—can be conceivably accomplished even if there is no fraternity. But this would be possible only by enforcing these through the strong arm of the state. However, if there is fraternity in society, then you don't need the state to enforce justice, liberty, equality: instead, these become the natural order of things.

Bandhuta is therefore the single most precious idea of the Constitution, but also the hardest to accomplish. So many people teach us hate—our leaders, our peers, our elders, our heroes from films and sports, our friends. We need instead teachers, leaders, philosophers, writers, film-makers, singers, artists, friends and family who teach us love.

Remember, it is not a country founded on hate, fear, division and inequality which we, the people of India promised to build. The country we gave to ourselves was a humane and equal country founded on love. Bandhuta is what brings us together as one country. We are not one country because we are alike. We are one country because, despite every difference in the way we look, eat, dress, speak, worship, love and think, we belong to and with each other. If there are shackles on your feet, I feel my freedom has been stolen. If you sleep hungry, I am unable to sleep. If your suffer loss and pain, tears well up in my eyes.

## Our Reality

But what is our reality? Look around. It is apparent that 'we, the people of India' have built a country still far distant from the India we promised ourselves in our constitution. And in some ways this distance is only growing.

Think of which of the magnificent and solemn pledges that we made to ourselves have been realized. What has become of the dreams of our founding mothers and fathers?

A great deal has indeed been accomplished. Every person in this country continues to hold the power to choose her government. Citizens of a large majority of newly independent countries were denied or lost this power, to military coups and dictators. Fewer people in our country are poor, fewer sleep hungry than when we won our freedom. The average length of life has risen from 37 years in 1947 to 67 years three quarters of a century later. We have some fine institutions for teaching the humanities, engineering, medicine and management, our warehouses are overloaded with food grains, we are the IT back office of the world, and our cities glitter with gated colonies, luxury cars and crowded malls.

But look carefully, and you will find that one in every third child is still malnourished. This means that their bodies and brains are not allowed to develop to full potential for lack of nutritious food and clean water. Children of the poor study in separate, significantly less resourced schools than children of the rich. Many are not allowed to study at all, and instead parents still feel compelled to send them out to hard labour. Every second woman in anaemic. Eight out of ten doctors in India work for for-profit private hospitals, and government spending on health care in India is among the lowest in the world. If poor people fall ill, they cannot rely on good quality publicly provisioned health care. Wealth accumulates in an incredibly small numbers of hands, and this is barely taxed. At the other far end of the spectrum, nine out of ten workers toil in casual, insecure, unsafe jobs at dirt wages. As they age, most have barely enough pensions to secure their aging with dignity and health care.

People still suffer horrible violence and discrimination because of their religion, caste and gender; or because they walk the paths of equality that is their right; or when they choose to love and marry outside the socially prescribed boundaries of religion, caste and gender. Adivasis are dispossessed by large powerful corporations from their forests and homelands, and are branded as Maoists and jailed when they protest. Crowds gather and lynch Muslim and Dalit men, beating them to death, and proudly videograph these crimes and circulate these on social media. Untouchability continues with pitiless and ferocious violence. Dalits are beaten and killed in India even today for growing a moustache, for building a two-storied house, for asking for fair wages, for just advancing in life through their own hard work and talent; their children thrashed for drinking water from an earthen pot meant for their 'high-caste' teacher. And these horrific crimes are rarely punished.

Governments punish instead people who disagree with them. The freedom to dissent is dying, with fear and official targeting choking voices of truth. The freedom of religious faith is threatened by the politics of majoritarian hate. People spend years in prison because they are too poor to afford legal counsel, because the courts are clogged and uncaring, because they belong to stigmatized religious and caste identities, or simply because they dare to challenge the injustices of the state.

Reflect on the essence, the morality, the soul of our constitution. It is not perfect. With the hindsight of history, there are some things we might want to change. But contained in it are the iridescent dreams we had for this nation when it threw off its chains of slavery. These are the ambitions, the lofty and worthy goals that we, the people set for our country. And since these are promises which we have made unto ourselves, it is for you and I, 'we, the people of India', to rebuild this country into the kind, equal, free and just land imagined by our founding mothers and fathers.

We must build with the bricks of our hearts and minds, of our dreams and our struggles, of our accomplishments and our sacrifices, and I hope, of love.

## This Series

India recently celebrated seventy-five years of its Independence. As one small tribute to the Indian freedom struggle, we propose a series of ten books that summarize in simple, accessible language the core values, imagination and pledges of the Constitution. The themes for these books we have been drawn mainly from the Preamble—Secularism, Socialism, Democracy, Justice, Liberty, Equality, Fraternity. In addition, we include the themes Scientific Temper and Federalism; these too are essential to the morality of the Indian Constitution. We are fortunate that the fine minds and hearts who we approached—some senior, some younger—all agreed generously to contribute to this series.

These books draw from the Constituent Assembly debates, and indeed from those that preceded them. Each book also looks at how these ideas evolved in independent India, through court rulings and executive actions. The series also looks at the relevance of these ideas to the challenges of the India of today, the extent to which the state, the polity, the economy and society remain faithful to these ideas, the principal contestations to these ideas, and finally, the ways in which these ideas are important for India's future as a humane, democratic state.

Dr Neera Chandhoke, one of India's leading political scientists, and Distinguished Fellow of the Centre for Equity Studies, consented to help me bring out the series and has also written this opening book for it. Ravi Singh, co-founder of Speaking Tiger and one of India's finest editors agreed to publish this series. We hope to get these translated into Hindi and other Indian languages as well.

At a time when the morality and pledges of the Constitution are under assault, it is our fervent wish that this small project—an effort to unpack and popularize it—will be useful as resistance, defence and public affirmation of the luminous morality of the founding document of India.

'India's Constitution bore the imprint of a long nationalist movement that made choices that have shaped its trajectory. The first and most significant choice was the idea of constitutionalism itself. The Indian national movement, while radical in its normative hopes, was self-consciously a constitutional movement.'

—Sujit Choudhry, Madhav Khosla and Pratap Bhanu Mehta, 'Locating Indian Constitutionalism', in *The Oxford Handbook of the Indian Constitution* (2016)

# Introduction

## *Why We Need the Indian Constitution*

We know the value of universal adult franchise because we have read long histories of struggles for it across the world. We also know how vulnerable people are in societies that have dispensed with a constitution. We are aware that the franchise empowers us as human beings and as citizens. To put it simply, it gives us agency.

But it is an undeniable fact that, in India's post-Independence history, upper-caste/class groups have prevented the so-called lower castes from exercising their franchise solely on the grounds of caste/class.

So imagine the following scenario: a Dalit woman is prevented from casting her vote in the general elections. Her constitutional right to vote as promised under Article 326 of the Constitution has been violated. Her status as a citizen has been diminished. What can our fellow citizen do to recover her rights?

She can reclaim her basic right to vote by appealing, with the help of civil liberty associations, to the judiciary. The case is serious enough for courts to rule remedial justice. Note that, just as it has granted her the right, the relevant provision of the Constitution has protected the right of our fellow citizen against muscular and unwarranted aggression of upper-caste/class men on election day.

Take the example of the acclaimed web series, *Dahaad*, created by Zoya Akhtar and Rima Kagti, where the police inspector Anjali, played to perfection by Sonakshi Sinha, is prevented by an 'upper caste' man from entering his mansion for official purposes. He cites her 'lower' caste as reason enough. Towards the end of the series, Anjali tells the caste-bound man, with considerable authority, that she has the right to enter his house to carry out police investigations simply because the *Constitution allows her to do so*. He is left dumbfounded, and Anjali confidently proceeds with her task of unmasking 'fake news', inflammable speeches, and, what are called in contemporary India, allegations of love jihad. This is the power of the Constitution—it gives us agency and therefore a sense of self-respect.

Let us think through the concept of agency. The notion of agency refers to the ability to conceptualize and live our lives the way we want to, driven by our goals and our ambitions. If a girl child wants to pursue higher studies because she wants to be a scientist, a writer, an educator, an artist, a theatre actor, or just study for the sake of educating her mind, no one should prevent her from doing so. Autonomous human beings should not allow people in power to decide what we should wear, what we should eat, who young people should marry, what our preferences, aspirations and desires ought to be. This is necessary if we want to live a good life, and who does not want to live a life that is worth living?

But this by itself is not enough. If philosophy tells us how to lead a good life, political philosophy tells us that a good life can be lived only in a good society. A good society is foremost a society that is organized into a constitutional democratic state based on universal adult franchise. This, we, as the people of India who have given to ourselves a constitution, have to protect. Politics, which establishes the rules of the game we call democracy, is too important to be left to professional politicians! We can intervene if our constitutional democratic state is under threat because we have the right to elect and dismiss governments. A profound principle of political philosophy is encoded in the concept of universal franchise. Every citizen has equal standing in society and her voice counts as much as anyone else's when it comes to political decision-making. The right to vote into power our rulers establishes the political competence of every citizen to participate in political affairs.

The principle of universal adult franchise also establishes the responsibility of representatives to the electorate. Our representatives in the government are obliged to provide the preconditions for, say, a girl child to educate herself by the provision of educational institutions, public libraries and book shops. She will not be able to pursue her dreams if the government censors books, bans education for girls or stipulates that they should stay at home. The basic precondition of a good life are thus obvious: the establishment of a public schooling system that imparts excellent affordable education and health care, but also opportunities for personal advancement. This is our right.

At the heart of every modern democracy lies a bill of rights which serves to limit the power of the state and therefore reinforce our status as people who count and count equally. If either the government or sections of society, bloated by their wealth and status as belonging to an upper caste and/or class, deny to vulnerable Indians their basic constitutional rights, they have not merely violated the Constitution, but harmed our democracy as well.

But we cannot stop at this. If constitutions protect citizens, citizens should protect the constitution from over-ambitious politicians who seek to accumulate power through centralization of authority and suppression of people's rights, or from judiciaries that kneel before their power. No individual is, however, able to challenge power by herself, particularly when the constitution has been compromised. Citizens must come together in webs of solidarity to take on powerful governments for their own rights, and the rights of their fellow citizens. Central to what we call civil society are social associations—civil liberty groups, women's associations and movements against caste and class oppressions. Our Dalit fellow citizen, who was prevented from casting her vote, for example, will likely approach the judiciary with the help of one or several such associations.

Citizens must come together to this end for the simple reason that they own the Constitution. Bring to mind the politically charged words of the Preamble:

> WE, THE PEOPLE OF INDIA having solemnly resolved to constitute India into a SOVEREIGN SOCIALIST SECULAR DEMOCRATIC REPUBLIC and to secure to all its citizens:

> JUSTICE, social, economic and political;
>
> LIBERTY of thought, expression, belief, faith and worship;
>
> EQUALITY of status and of opportunity; and to promote among them all
>
> FRATERNITY assuring the dignity of the individual and the unity and integrity of the Nation;
>
> IN OUR CONSTITUENT ASSEMBLY this twenty-sixth day of November, 1949, do HEREBY ADOPT, ENACT AND GIVE TO OURSELVES THIS CONSTITUTION.

The moment we recognize that we *own* the Constitution, our perspective changes. Our foundational document must not be misused or dispensed with by power hungry and cynical politicians who, in Oscar Wilde's words, 'know the price of everything and the value of nothing'. The Constitution of India is the people's constitution, and 'we, the people' should stand with each other to defend it against anyone who threatens to dispense with it, or rewrite it. The sentiment which enables us to stand together is solidarity, or fraternity.

The meaning of solidarity is best summed up by the Russian poet Anna Akhmatova's famous poem, *Requiem*. In the 1930s, thousands of Russians were rounded up and sent to the Gulag. Anna spent seventeen months waiting in long queues outside a jail in Leningrad to find out what had happened to her son. She began the *Requiem* with these heart-rending lines: 'No, not under a foreign sky / Nor in the shelter of a foreign wing / With my people there stood I / With them in their suffering'. Suffering with our people is what sympathy and solidarity are about.

What we must not forget is that the Constitution of India is the product of legislation and judicial interpretation but also of a mass struggle that fostered this solidarity. Just as importantly, it was Indians who actually *wrote* the Constitution. While some constitutions of the former British colonies were written by constituent assemblies, these ultimately had to be approved by the British colonial power before they became independent. This was particularly the case with African countries that joined the British Commonwealth—Ghana, Nigeria, Kenya and Tanganyika. Their constitutions were granted by the British monarch by the same stroke that granted them independence. Belgian officials dictated the constitutional path towards independence in Burundi, and played an important role in the constitution of the former Belgian Congo. The constitutions of Asian countries were partially written by the British or their appointees. The constitution of Malaysia, for example, was drafted by a committee that was appointed by the British Crown, and chaired by the British jurist, Lord Reid. There was no constituent assembly set up in the country. Sir Ivor Jennings, a lawyer and academic, practically drafted the constitution of Sir Lanka.[1]

Our constitution was not written by the colonial power. In fact, the demand that Indians should write their own constitution came up fairly early in the freedom struggle. Inspired and led by visionary leaders like M.K. Gandhi, it was one of the greatest struggles for freedom the world witnessed in the twentieth century. Where in today's world will we find a Gandhi who was willing to lay down his life to save a Muslim under attack? Who has the competence to rewrite a constitution forged through decades of struggle? This is what the Indian people should ask when politicians talk about rewriting the Constitution. We should be able to tell them: *This Constitution is ours and we will defend it!*

If follows, and this is the theme of this essay, that we should think of the Constitution as not only a legal but a political and a normative document which establishes the values according to which our polity is to be run, which establishes a relationship between the state and the people, and which, significantly, establishes a relationship between the people themselves.

In the pages that follow, I focus on some of the most important issues that constitute the bedrock of our democratic Constitution. As a starting point, I detail the making of the Constitution by the leaders of the freedom struggle, the genesis of the Constitution in documents that date back to 1895, and the insistence that it should be written *by Indians* in a Constituent Assembly elected on the principle of *universal adult franchise*. We find that it was the values upheld by this struggle that ultimately made their way into the Constitution; it was written by the same women and men who led the movement.

Specifically, I detail two issues that were of prime concern to the makers of the Constitution.

First, in a multi-religious society, the principle of secularism is of enormous significance. It is so because it is an offshoot of the principle of equality: that all are entitled to be treated as equals by the state. No one should be advantaged or disadvantaged because of reasons outside her control, such as birth into a community that is in a minority in the country. Secularism is an extension of equality because it establishes the principle that the state should treat all *religions* as equal. All people, irrespective of the religious community they are born into, have to be free, but more importantly, they have to be equally free. This has been established by the Supreme Court; we also see it being elaborated much earlier by Pandit Jawaharlal Nehru.

Yet, and this is the second focus, in a highly inegalitarian society, people can neither be free nor equal if they lack access to what the philosopher John Rawls called primary goods. A hungry person cannot be a free person. Hunger, and its main cause, poverty, prevent the citizen from realizing, or even conceptualizing, the good life. Without these primary goods, political and civil rights—e.g. the right to vote, the right to contest elections, freedom of expression, the right to form associations, the right to liberty and the right to dissent—will remain at the level of formal rights. They cannot be secured unless people have access to social rights—the right to employment, the right to health, the right to education, the right to housing and the right to food. In the Constitution, social rights were placed in chapter four, in Directive Principles of State Policy, rather than chapter three which details our Fundamental Rights. A series of civil society movements and a sometimes supportive Supreme Court ensured that some of these principles of state policy were upgraded to the status of rights. We see here an interesting interplay between state policy and civil society in the making of social rights.

And this brings me to the rationale of the final chapter on social movements. Democracy gives us the bare outlines of a system where every individual is treated as someone who counts equally. Rights in this sense shape the form and content of democracy. But *democracy is a project*, and it can be furthered, if not completed, by social movements that stress the expansion of the right to vote to hitherto marginalized constituencies, the right not to be displaced from their habitat for big projects, the right of women to ancestral property, the right of the queer community to same-sex relationships, protection of the right to civil liberties, the right of people to a sound environment, the right to live in dignity, and above all the right to hold a government responsible for acts of omission and commission.

Secularism, equal freedoms, redistribution and social movements, to my mind, form the core of democracy. No one who is not committed to freedom, equality and secularism, and resultantly justice and solidarity can be called democratic. No society can call itself democratic if it discriminates against minorities, no society can call itself a democracy if its people remain hungry, and certainly no society can describe itself as such if the right to form associations and the freedom of expression in civil society is truncated by governments. This introduction to the Constitution touches upon many of these issues, leaving an elaboration on these and many others to other authors in the series.

## Chapter I

# The Making of the Constitution

The renowned legal scholar Professor G. Mohan Gopal succinctly sums up the struggle for the Indian Constitution. 'Three powerful competing and mutually conflicting ideologies,' he believes, 'battled in the Constituent Assembly to capture the idea of India: feudal theocracy, modernity, and swaraj. While the last two have considerable common ground there are important differences. Swaraj was more than a demand for independence from the British or for the wholesale adoption of modernity. It was a demand from common people for grassroots representative democracy, roaring down like a mighty river from centuries of struggle of the marginalized populations of India for their due share of power. Each of these forces have left a deep imprint on the Constitution. But the soul of the Constitution is the unique imprint of the mass movement for swaraj. Without it, we would not have had the Preamble, Part III and Part IV in their present form.'[2]

Indeed, Indian democracy was not invented by a random

group of people who met in the elegant environs of what was to become the parliament of the new nation. Except for some members who were invited by Jawaharlal Nehru and others to join the Assembly, because they were legal experts, or because they represented significant shades of opinion, a majority of members were veterans of the national movement. They had participated in the making of various constitutional drafts, and they knew what a society that had mobilized for independence expected from the government of an independent India.

Every significant political initiative/event is the outcome of multiple strands of history. 'Nothing comes of nothing', says Lear to his daughter Cordelia in the first act of Shakespeare's *King Lear*. Shakespeare reiterated a dictum first offered by the Greek philosopher Parmenides. Our Constitution was the outcome of a complex interweaving of historical developments; the aspirations of the national movement, constitutional legislation passed by the colonial power, and the constitutional history of other countries—France, England, US, Ireland and Greece among others.

### Inaugurating the Process

On 9 December 1946, the Constituent Assembly met in the central hall of the magnificent famed circular building of what was until then the seat of the Imperial Legislative Council in Delhi. The Objectives Resolution, which spelt out the aims of the Constituent Assembly, was introduced by Pandit Jawaharlal Nehru. Nehru took care to emphasize that the Assembly was not a gift of the colonial government. It was the upshot of a number of initiatives taken by the leaders of the Indian National Congress; the product of the intellectual labour of Indian jurists and public intellectuals, and also the outcome of numerous political compromises. Collectively, these initiatives had smote the fundamental principles of a democratic polity onto a political stone since the turn of the twentieth century. Introducing the Resolution in the Assembly on 13 December 1946, Pandit Nehru memorably remarked: 'For a long time we have been having various plans for a free India in our minds, but now, when we are beginning the actual work, I hope, you will be at one with me when I say, that we should present a clear picture of this plan to ourselves, to the people of India and to the world at large.'[3]

He added, in his inimitably elegant prose, 'Words are magic things often enough, but even the magic of words sometimes cannot convey the magic of the human spirit and of a Nation's passion. And so, I cannot say that this Resolution at all conveys the passion that lies in the hearts and the minds of the Indian people today. It seeks very feebly to tell the world of what we have thought or dreamt of so long, and what we now hope to achieve in the near future.'[4]

What the makers of the Constitution wished to achieve was nothing less than stupendous, the transformation of society, of the polity and of the economy after 200 years of colonial rule. The soul of the Constitution was the charter of the fundamental rights of the people of India, the institutionalization of checks on the exercise of power, the division of power, representative democracy and popular sovereignty.

Our constitution can hardly be conceptualized in abstraction from history or the political context of the times. Admittedly, it borrowed from other constitutions in the world. It could not have been otherwise. India was a relative latecomer to constitution-making. The makers naturally looked to other democratic constitutions for inspiration and guidance.

The learned Dr Ambedkar, the chairman of the Drafting Committee of the Constitution, acknowledged as much. On 4 November 1948, he addressed a set of significant criticisms that had been catapulted onto the agenda of the Assembly: one of them being that the provisions of the Constitution had been taken from the West. Can a constitution, he asked rhetorically, framed in the middle of the twentieth century be absolutely new? 'The only new things, if there can be any,' he said, 'in a constitution framed so late in the day are the variations made to remove the faults and to accommodate it to the needs of the country... As to the accusation that the Draft Constitution has produced a good part of the provisions of the Government of India Act, 1935 [passed by the British Parliament to grant a greater measure of autonomy to Indians], I make no apologies. There is nothing to be ashamed of in borrowing. It involves no plagiarism.'[5]

At the same time, the preamble to our Constitution is shot through by a strong and vibrant political commitment to the objectives of the freedom struggle: freedom and justice, equality and fraternity. The Preamble could not possibly have been written by a colonial power. The colonial government had rejected the idea of fundamental rights for Indians right up to the British Cabinet Mission Plan in 1946. It was only then that the Plan advised the setting up of an Advisory Committee for

Fundamental Rights and Minority Rights. These were the very rights that had been demanded by the leaders of the freedom struggle and public intellectuals since the early decades of the twentieth century.

## A Brief Account of Constitution-making in India

In 1895, the draft of a 'Constitution of India Bill' came to the attention of the political public. No one seemed to know who had authored the Bill, though Annie Besant believed that Lokmanya Tilak had drafted it. The constitutional draft focalized civil rights: the right to express one's thought in words or writing, and the right to publish them without liability to censure. It further laid down that under the provisions of the Bill of Rights, nobody could be imprisoned unless a specific crime had been proved against him according to law, that no one could be sentenced except by a competent authority, the law should be equal for all, and that every citizen had the right to property and the right to elect one member to the Parliament of India, and one to the Local Legislative Council.[6] In a brief preface dated 8 May 1895, the author admitted that at that time the people of India were 'far from being able to exercise the rights proposed to be conferred' upon them. He/she, however, hoped that 'under the benign Government of the British' they would 'in future be able to enjoy and use them to the greatest advantage of their country and the British Government'.[7]

It was still too early in the day for nationalists to think of independence. The Indian National Congress, which was established in 1885 concentrated on the politics of petition-making till the second decade of the twentieth century. That was the politically momentous moment when Gandhi arrived on the scene of Indian politics and transformed the freedom struggle.

Expectations and ambitions changed rapidly from thereon. As early as 1919, a considerable section of nationalist opinion came to believe that it was vital that the Constitution of India should be framed by Indians themselves.[8] A series of initiatives towards this end culminated in a conference held in Delhi in February 1923 attended by members of the central and provincial legislatures. The conference outlined the essentials of a constitution, placing India on a plane of equality with the self-governing dominions of the British Empire. The draft was discussed, edited and amended in a series of meetings.

The final draft of the Commonwealth of India Bill, 1925 that was put forward held that India had the right to self-government, that it should be placed on an equal footing with Self-Governing Dominions, and that it should possess the same responsibilities and privileges. It developed the list of rights first enumerated in the 1895 Bill. A Declaration of Rights stated that every person had the fundamental right to liberty of person and security of his dwelling and property, freedom of conscience, free profession and practice of religion, the free expression of opinion and the right to assemble peacefully and without arms. Each person had the right to form associations and unions. The Bill provided for the right to free elementary education, gender equality, and equality before the law irrespective of any consideration of nationality.[9]

In May 1925, the Bill was sent to D. Graham Pole, who was a friend of Annie Besant, an influential member of the Labour

Party and the then Secretary of the British Committee on Indian Affairs. It was accompanied by a memorandum signed by forty-three influential Indian political leaders of various parties. The memorandum asked for Dominion status and claimed the right of self-determination: 'Resentment is justly felt in India against Britain because of the refusal of Britain to apply in India the principles for which India and Britain fought shoulder to shoulder in the war.'[10]

In England, the Bill titled 'A Bill to constitute within the British Empire a Commonwealth of India' was carefully revised by Labour Party leaders Henry Slesser and Arthur Henderson. It found wide support in the Labour Party and was accepted unanimously by the Executive Committee of the Parliamentary Labour Party. It then had its first reading in the House of Commons in December 1925, and in the same month the House ordered that it may be printed. However, with the defeat of the Labour Party, the fate of the Bill was sealed.

About two years later, at the Madras session of the Indian National Congress in 1927, the party decided to draft a constitution in association with other political groups. A committee was appointed by the All India Parties Conference at its meeting in Bombay on 19 May 1928. The mandate of the committee was to consider and determine the principles of a draft constitution for independent India. The heightened tensions between the Hindu and Muslim communities added to the significance of the establishment of the committee. There was a need to resolve the communal issue and the question of Dominion status under the British. The chairman of the committee was Motilal Nehru.[11]

Among various recommendations in the Motilal Nehru Committee draft constitution, the committee clearly stated that 'All powers of government and all authority legislative, executive and judicial are derived from the people'.[12] The draft drew up an elaborate list of rights. The constitutional scholar Granville Austin, who has authored two definitive books on the Indian Constitution, suggests that the rights granted by the Nehru Report were a close precursor to the fundamental rights chapter of the Constitution. Ten of the nineteen sub-clauses reappeared materially unchanged, and three of the Nehru Report rights are included in the Directive Principles.[13]

The expanse of fundamental rights written into the Nehru draft constitution was remarkable in more senses than one. Foremost on the list was a right that is basic to democracy—universal adult franchise. The Nehru Report stated that any artificial restriction on the right to vote in a democratic constitution is an unwarranted restriction on democracy itself. For, whenever the body of voters is limited, welfare excludes individuals. There is no equation, the recommendations suggested, between civic virtue or literacy and the possession of the franchise. In the opinion of the Committee, the repeated exercise of the right to vote is in itself a powerful educative factor: 'We attach no weight to the objections based on the prevailing illiteracy of the masses and their lack of political experience... Political experience can only be acquired by an active participation in political institutions and does not entirely depend upon literacy. There should be equal opportunities available to all to acquire this experience.'[14] The rates of non-literacy have been going down in India, but in absolute terms a large number of Indians are still non-literate. This does not preclude the grant of universal adult franchise. If the Motilal Nehru Constitutional Draft had not dismissed a posited necessary relationship between literacy and the franchise, large numbers of Indians would have been excluded from the body politic. The constitutional grant of universal adult franchise therefore protected the political rights of the marginalized.

Western theorists of democracy count a middle class and literacy as two of the basic preconditions of democracy. The Nehru Report established that it is not literacy but participation in political affairs that enables a people to make the transition from subjects to citizens. Nor can universal adult franchise be restricted to women over a certain age. This was a welcome improvement on Western theories of democracy that had granted the vote to women late in the day. Note how universal adult franchise was not invented in the Constituent Assembly set up in 1946. It was part of the demands of the freedom struggle and was codified in constitutional documents authored by nationalists.

The right to vote was followed by a list of fundamental rights: '[N]o person shall be deprived of his liberty, nor shall his dwelling or property be entered, sequestered or confiscated save in accordance with law... [All citizens shall have] the right of free expression of opinion, as well as the right to assemble peaceably and without arms, and to form associations or unions...for purposes not opposed to public law and morality...' The right to equality before the law was another important right, particularly for a supremely unequal society.[15] Significantly, minorities were granted the right to their religion and cultural practices.

Among others, Gandhi appreciated the labour that had gone into the making of the report. 'And if the practical unanimity arrived at after strenuous labours by the Committee is sealed by the Conference about to meet in Lucknow,' he wrote, 'a tremendous step will have been taken in the direction of constitutional swaraj as distinguished from what might be termed organic swaraj... In thus commending this report to the public, I tender my congratulations to Pandit Motilal Nehru without whose effort there would have been no Committee, there would have been no unanimity and there would have been no report.'[16] The report of the draft constitution was unanimously accepted by the All Parties Conference with a few modifications.

In March 1933, the British government issued a White Paper containing proposals for constitutional reforms in India. These were subsequently, with some modifications, included in the Government of India Act, 1935. In June 1934, the Indian National Congress demanded that the colonial government, as part of its official policy, set up a constituent assembly elected on the basis of universal adult franchise to draft a constitution. For the first time, the demand for a constituent assembly was made formally. The Congress Working Committee rejected the 1933 White Paper, because it did not represent the will of the people of India. The CWC stated that the 'only satisfactory alternative to the White Paper is a constitution drawn up by a Constituent Assembly elected on the basis of adult suffrage or as near to it as possible, with the power, if necessary, to the important minorities to have their representatives elected exclusively by the electors belonging to such minorities'.[17] Witness the political sagacity of the leaders of the freedom movement. They not only wanted that Indians should write their own constitution, but also that representatives of minorities should be elected exclusively by electors belonging to the community.

Underlying the resolution was the belief that the people of India could feel that they owned the constitution only if it was written and signed by their representatives, and not by officials of the colonial power. In a piece titled 'The Only Way', which appeared in the *Harijan* of 19 November 1939, Gandhi wrote that 'Pandit Jawaharlal Nehru has compelled me to study, among other things, the implications of a Constituent Assembly... Hard facts have, however, made me a convert and, for that reason, perhaps more enthusiastic than Jawaharlal himself. For I seem to see in it a remedy which Jawaharlal may not, for our communal and other distempers, besides being a vehicle for mass political and other education'.[18]

Gandhi went on to write that only a constituent assembly could produce a constitution that was indigenous, and that was representative of the will of the people. It would not be ideal, but it would be real howsoever much it might appear imperfect in the eyes of legal luminaries. Self-government had to represent the will of the people. The people might make a hash of governing themselves but they could not govern themselves through a government imposed from without 'even as the fable jackdaw could not walk like a peacock with feathers borrowed from his elegant companion'.[19]

Reportedly one of the longest pieces of legislation passed by the British parliament, the Government of India Act, 1935 came into effect in 1937. Parliamentary debates around the Act involved 2,000 speeches.[20] The Act created a federation of India that consisted of two levels: a central executive and parliament, and below it provinces and princely states. It introduced the idea of popularly elected provincial legislatures, established a federal court and gave the vote to 14 per cent of the putative electorate. Separate electorates were provided for Muslims, Sikhs and others though not for the Depressed Classes.

In a comprehensive resolution in April 1936, the Congress rejected in toto the Act and declared that no constitution imposed by an outside authority could be accepted. The Act, stated the resolution, 'in no way represents the will of the nation, [it] is designed to facilitate and perpetuate the domination and exploitation of the people of India and is imposed on the country to the accompaniment of widespread repression and the suppression of civil liberties'.[21] At his presidential address at the Faizpur Congress in December 1936, Nehru once again reiterated the demand for a Constituent Assembly elected under adult suffrage: 'This assembly must not be conceived as something emanating from the British Government or as a compromise with British imperialism...it must have the will of the people behind it and the organized strength of the masses to support it, and the power to draw up the constitution of a free India.'[22]

During the Second World War, the demand for a constituent assembly was again raised by Jawaharlal Nehru in a 1940 piece titled 'Why We Ask for a Constituent Assembly?' He wrote that if we aim for freedom there is no way out for us but a constituent assembly. A constitution authored by and for the people 'means the creation of a new state; it means the walking out and away from the economic foundations and structure of imperialism. This cannot be done by the wisest of lawyers sitting together in a conclave; it cannot be done by small committees trying to balance interests and calling that constitution-making; it cannot be done under the shadow of an external authority. It can only be done effectively when...the urge and the sanctions come from the masses. Hence the vital importance of adult suffrage'.[23]

Nehru's expectations and aspirations that the constituent assembly would be popularly elected were fated to disappointment. On 11 March 1940, British Prime Minister Winston Churchill announced to the House of Commons that the war cabinet had decided to promote a political settlement in India. On 29 March 1942, Sir Stafford Cripps, a member of the war cabinet, brought a set of proposals to India for discussion with the nationalist leaders.

The Draft Declaration of the British government accepted the demand that Indians should write their own constitution. It also recommended that the moment the war ended, steps would be taken to set up an elected body. However, the Congress Working Committee rejected the proposals. The Congress found the plan unsatisfactory in regard to the grouping of provinces, and the right of the European members of provincial assemblies to take part in the elections to the Constituent Assembly. The president of the Congress, Maulana Azad, wrote to the Secretary of State in May 1942, 'The Assembly itself, when formed, will in my committee's opinion, be a sovereign body for the purpose of drafting the constitution unhindered by any external authority...its final decisions will automatically take effect'.[24]

In early 1946, another Cabinet Mission of the British government arrived in India. The objective of the Mission was to mediate between the Congress and the Muslim League in order to build up some consensus on how the interests of both communities could be accommodated. The second objective of the Mission was to discuss the setting up of a constituent assembly.

On 16 May 1946, the Mission proposed that an interim government should be established to carry on the administration of British India till the time a new constitution was promulgated. The demand of the Muslim League that a portion of the territory of undivided India be carved out to create an independent state of Pakistan, however, was rejected. The Mission was of the opinion that '[t]he argument for a separate state of Pakistan was based, first, upon the right of the Muslim majority [in certain regions demanded by the Muslim League] to decide their method of Government according to their wishes, and secondly, upon the necessity to include substantial areas in which Muslims are in a minority, in order to make Pakistan administratively and economically workable... [T]he setting up of a separate sovereign State of Pakistan on the lines claimed by the Muslim League would not solve the communal minority problem; nor can we see any justification for including within a sovereign Pakistan those districts of the Punjab and of Bengal and Assam in which the population is predominantly non-Muslim. Every argument that can be used in favour of Pakistan can equally, in our view, be used in favour of the exclusion of the non-Muslim areas from Pakistan'.[25]

The alternative to the partition of India was the establishment of a three-tier federation—a federal centre, provincial groupings and individual provinces. The Union of India would, it was proposed, be constituted of both British India as well as the princely states, which were to 'retain all subjects and powers other than those ceded to the Union'. The central government would have restricted powers over foreign affairs, defence and communication. It would be given the power to raise finances for the administration of these subjects. All other subjects would remain with the provinces.

The provinces were free to form groups. Each group could set up an executive and a legislature with power over the provincial subjects common to the members of the group. But the constitutions of both the Union and the groups had to carry a provision that any province could, by a majority vote of its legislative assembly, call for a reconsideration of the terms of the constitution after the initial ten years, and at ten yearly intervals thereafter.[26] And finally, the Mission ruled out the principle of universal adult franchise for elections to the constituent assembly. The principle, accepted the Mission, was desirable, but impractical. It would delay the making of the constitution.

Instead, they proposed, provincial legislative assemblies should elect members to the constituent assembly. The total number of seats allotted to a province would be in proportion to its population; roughly in the ratio of one to a million. For the purposes of electing representatives to the constituent assembly, members of the provincial assemblies were grouped into three categories: General, Muslim and Sikh. Smaller minorities would be given full representation on all matters that were of special interest to them.[27]

By a resolution adopted on 25 June 1946, the Congress accepted the Cabinet Mission Plan. The Working Committee had examined the proposals both from the point of view of immediate independence, and the opening out of avenues leading to the rapid economic and social advance of the masses. The proposals fell short of many of the objectives of the Congress. Yet they were considered seriously by the Working Committee because the party desired an early and a peaceful settlement of the problem. This course of action would end the conflict between India and England. The Committee felt that the proposals strengthened the central government, ensured the right of a province to choose the group it wished to join and protected minorities.

The CWC ultimately decided that the Congress should participate in the proposed constituent assembly and frame the constitution of a free, united and democratic India. Further, that a representative and responsible provisional national government should be formed at the earliest possible date. 'The continuation of an authoritarian and unrepresentative Government can only add to the suffering of the famishing masses and increase discontent,' it was argued. 'It will also put in jeopardy,' continued the statement, 'the work of the Constituent Assembly, which can only function in a free environment.'[28] On 2 September 1946, an interim government was formed with Jawaharlal Nehru as the Vice President of the executive council.

## Within The Constituent Assembly

Elections to the 296 seats of the Constituent Assembly were held in July 1946. The Congress secured a majority. Among the members of the Assembly were men and women who had led the freedom struggle, and public intellectuals who had participated in deliberations on the future of the country: Jawaharlal Nehru, Bhimji Rao Ambedkar, Govind Ballabh Pant, Rafi Ahmad Kidwai, C. Rajagopalachari and others. Among members nominated by the Congress were Frank Reginald Anthony representing the Ango-Indian community, Shyama Prasad Mukherjee, the president of the All India Hindu Mahasabha, Jagjivan Ram, president of the All-India Depressed Classes League, and Ms Hansa Mehta, president of the All-India Women's Conference.

Indirect elections to the Constituent Assembly were based on the restricted franchise enumerated in the Sixth Schedule of the 1935 Government of India Act. The franchise excluded the mass of peasants, the majority of shop keepers and traders, workers and countless others from the rolls by tax, property and educational qualifications. Only 28.5 per cent of the adult population of the provinces was entitled to vote in the 1946 provincial elections. This formed the social base of the Constituent Assembly.

The leadership was disappointed that its demand that the Assembly should be elected through universal adult franchise had not been met. Nevertheless, the atmosphere in which it met was charged with excitement. The leaders of the freedom movement had not only demanded independence; they had thought out carefully the normative basis of the political community that would form the fulcrum of the Constitution. Over the years, they had established the basic principles of democracy: the rights of the people, limited powers of the government and its obligations to the people of India. After 200 years, India would finally be free. It was time to put into practice the thinking, the debates and the reflections of the leaders of the freedom struggle. It was time to realize the commitments that had been made to the people during the struggle. It was time to realize azaadi or swaraj.

The task before the Assembly was clearly not an easy one. Jawaharlal Nehru movingly articulated the predicament while presenting the Objectives Resolution: 'We are at the end of an era and possibly very soon we shall embark upon a new age; and my mind goes back to the great past of India, to the 5,000 years of India's history... All that past crowds around me, and exhilarates me, and, at the same time, somewhat oppresses me. Am I worthy of that past?'

'When I think also of the future,' continued Nehru, 'the greater future I hope, standing on this sword's edge of the present between this mighty past and the mightier future, I tremble a little and feel overwhelmed by this mighty task. We have come here at a strange moment in India's history. I do not know but I do feel that there is some magic in this moment of transition from the old to the new, something of that magic which one sees when the night turns into day and even though the day may be a cloudy one, it is day after all, for when the clouds move away, we can see the sun later on... [W]e have big things to face, big things to say and big things to do...'[29]

The clouds did not move away completely because the Muslim League did not join the Constituent Assembly in December 1946. The Assembly, hoping that it would, postponed discussions on the Objectives Resolution till January 1947.

But the League, now reasonably certain that it would secure a state of its own, refused to participate. The Muslim population represented by the Muslim League went unrepresented in the Assembly. Represented were those Muslims that preferred to be led by secular leaders like Maulana Azad.

Given the absence of the Muslim League, the Constituent Assembly was dominated by the Congress, which also formed the interim government. Yet, as Granville Austin observes, decision-making in the Constituent Assembly was democratic. Congress members covered a broad ideological spectrum and represented the diverse viewpoints of voters and non-voters alike.[30] At the same time, the party lent coherence to the deliberations. On 25 November 1949, Dr Ambedkar acknowledged that the task of the Drafting Committee would have been very difficult if the Assembly had been merely 'a motley crowd, a tessellated pavement without cement, a black stone here and a white stone there... There would have been nothing but chaos'. The Congress party brought into the proceedings a sense of order and discipline. 'The Congress party is, therefore, entitled to all the credit for the smooth sailing of the Draft Constitution in the Assembly.'[31]

The central leadership of the Congress did not interfere in the selection of representatives to the provincial assemblies. But the High Command attempted to ensure that persons of exceptional ability were chosen and also that minorities were represented. The Cabinet Mission Plan had only made provisions for Sikhs and Muslim minorities but the party took care to ensure that representatives from among the Parsis, Anglo-Indians, Indian Christians, members of the Scheduled

Castes and Tribes, and women were brought into the Assembly as part of the General category.[32]

It was a time to realize dreams of freedom, but also to recognize the internal tensions that had erupted alongside, and often within, the freedom struggle. Recent events had sent tremors of disquiet along the spines of the makers of the Constitution. Fear that the country would be further Balkanized influenced many decisions that had to be reversed later, for example, the issue of creating units of the federal system on the basis of language. (The demand for linguistic states was accepted later in 1953 after a sustained agitation. The States Reorganisation Act was passed in 1956.) These fears buttressed the argument for a strong central government.

A strong central government was also needed for the transformation from agitational politics to a democratic political society, to hold together a nation which had been split apart by the Partition, and to provide for the wellbeing of the people. The Constituent Assembly set the tone for this. During the period of the drafting of the Constitution, India was partitioned on the basis of religion. Yet minorities were granted the right to their own religion, practices, education and language. The leaders hoped for a new society that was based on civic responsibility. For India had passed through a storm of communal hatred which led to division of not only territory but hearts, minds and sensibilities.

The makers of the Constitution had recognized that their society was buffeted by a number of injustices. Among these, two appeared intractable. The first was a double disadvantage, i.e. economic deprivation as well as social discrimination, which vulnerable communities such as the Scheduled Castes and Tribes were subjected to. The second problem was the demonization of that section of the Muslim minority that had opted to stay back in India. The challenge before the democratic state was to secure justice for these groups. The Assembly opted for redistributive justice and affirmative action on the one hand, and minority rights on the other. The Constitution in other words adopted the substantive notion of equality, that taking into account background inequalities, provides special measures for disadvantaged groups. This was a wise move, since these groups are often subjected to economic deprivation *because* they are socially discriminated against.

~

The 26th of January 1950, the day the Constitution came into effect as the linchpin of the Indian Republic, was, according to all reports, a day of great joy and enthusiasm for all those who had fought for the independence of India, and asserted the right of Indians to forge their own future. Understandably so. The constitution of the Indian Republic as well as of the new political community of 'we, the people', represented a culmination of decades of struggle. Hundreds of thousands, from diverse backgrounds, had been inspired by their leaders, public intellectuals, progressive writers and poets to come together and protest against colonial policies, demonstrate against unjust laws, readily go to prison and sacrifice their lives if necessary. It was their moment to celebrate.

Despite a rocky biography, that feeling of solidarity inspired by our leaders, intellectuals and poets has helped consolidate the political community forged by the Constitution in the seven decades that followed.

# Chapter II

# The Constitution, Democracy and Our Political Community

A constitution forms a bridge between the world of procedural politics regulated by law and the political community that clothes the dry bones of the law with sentiments. It follows that any political community that aspires to democracy cannot exist and reproduce itself independently of the legal provisions of the Constitution, or of the language of rights. It cannot exist independently of the powers of the state either. This is the contradiction that stalks democracy because power can truncate and even suppress rights. We can hardly think of a 'normal' political community in a society where debate is frowned upon, dissent is banned, activists are jailed and minorities are harassed. In such cases, the political community has to courageously gear up to defend fellow citizens.

Democratic constitutionalism falters if people do not care about others, about their ill health or about their poverty. And it is a fact that in many countries constitutions have been periodically dumped, replaced by another one, and subsequently replaced by yet another. In other countries, political elites have bended constitutions to their will, aided by complicit judiciaries and a media that abjectly kneels before power. In yet other cases, constitutions have been reduced to a husk, existing as mere camouflage for authoritarian governments. Since a constitution casts a veneer of legitimacy over the exercise of power and presents raw power as moral authority, it is considered desirable by even authoritarian rulers who yearn to be called democratic at home and abroad.

The thinking citizen will, however, agree that the state of democracy in a country is measured not by self-congratulatory statements by people in power, but by the kind of political community that obtains in that country. For ultimately, the constitution is protected not by people in power who tend to use its provisions cynically, but by members of the political community that the constitution itself has created.

## Non-democratic and Democratic Constitutions

Neither democracy nor constitutions are, of course, specific to modern times. Ancient Athens had initiated democracy in 500 BCE. The meaning of democracy was spelled out in the famous funeral oration given by the great Athenian statesman, Pericles—written into the history of the Peloponnesian War between the city-states of Athens and Sparta by the historian Thucydides—at the mass burial of fallen soldiers after the first year of battle. The funeral oration, an Athenian practice, offered the opportunity to skilled orators to mourn warriors who had given their life for the country, to acknowledge the contribution of their ancestors to the making of their culture and to defend democracy which gave an edge to Athenians over Spartans.

We should, said Pericles, remember and honour our ancestors who struggled to give us a free state and a great empire. 'Our constitution does not copy the laws of neighbouring states: we are rather a pattern to others than imitators ourselves. Its administration favours the many instead of the few; this is why it is called a democracy. If we look to the laws, they afford equal justice to all... The freedom which we enjoy in our government extends also to our ordinary life. [F]ar from exercising a jealous surveillance over each other, we do not feel called upon to be angry with our neighbour for doing what he likes'.

Note the disjuncture between theory and practice that plagues his otherwise brilliant exposition of democracy. Democracy was born in Athens; *demos* is after all a Greek word. But the privileges of democratic citizenship were reserved only for Athenian-born men. Women, slaves and men born in other countries did not have citizenship rights. Aristotle (384–322 BCE), considered to be the founder of the discipline of political science, which was for him the master science, collected and studied the constitutions of 158 city-states. Most of these city-states were hardly larger than some of our neighbourhoods, but they did possess constitutions that organized the way citizens lived and defined the power of the state. The idea of universal adult franchise was, however, unknown to the makers of these constitutions, or indeed to Aristotle.

This disjuncture between citizens and non-citizens initially plagued the democracies set up in France, the United States and the United Kingdom in the eighteenth century, when the history of modern constitutions was inaugurated. In the United States of America, the constitution written at the Philadelphia Convention in 1787, and ratified by a majority of states that subsequently formed a federation, took effect in 1788. In France, the Declaration of the Rights of Man and the Citizen, made after the fall of the Bastille prison during the French Revolution of 1789, formed the preamble to the Constitution enacted in 1791.

The US constitution marked a formal and legal break of the country from Britain. In France, the constitution heralded a new age free from the oppressive regime of the monarchy which had been brought to an inglorious end by the 1789 revolution. In both cases, the new constitution followed the overthrow of the previous regime—a colonial power in the case of the USA, and the monarchical regime in France.

Initially, the English, the French and the American constitutions, despite their emphasis on universality, did not grant the right to vote to women. Women had to fight for the franchise. This was granted after sustained mobilization only in the first half of the twentieth century. In England, every adult woman got the vote in 1928, in the USA in 1920 and in France in 1944. In Greece, which is the birthplace of democracy, women got the right to vote only in 1952.

By the middle of the twentieth century, the arrival of newly decolonized states onto the world stage was marked by an explosion of constitution-making. The post-colonial world looked to India, which adopted its democratic constitution in 1950. This was accomplished despite the fact that the country did not meet the requirements set by Western theorists for democracy: literacy, a middle class, economic wellbeing, cultural homogeneity and a civic culture. As we have seen, the Motilal Nehru Constitutional Draft, written by the leaders of the freedom struggle in 1928, institutionalized universal adult franchise. Women, or the so-called lower castes, or the working classes did not have to *fight* for the vote. In any case, it is absurd to assume that leaders of mass movements, sitting down to write a constitution, would coolly and cynically debate whether the masses should get the vote. Indians were willing to lay down their lives for independence. If they were not fighting for a democratic India, what were they fighting for?

But a dilemma stalks democracy. Modern constitutions are distinct from earlier ones because they are based on popular sovereignty and fundamental rights of citizens. The opening phrase of the Preamble of the Indian Constitution, 'We, the People of India', reinforces the doctrine of popular sovereignty: ultimately, power rests with the people. An inchoate but politically charged entity called 'the people' *delegates* power to a democratically elected government. Yet governments, howsoever democratically they may be elected, have an inherent tendency to accumulate and augment power at the expense of people's rights.

The path to democracy is thus strewn with pitfalls. For one, there is little connection between political democracy and social democracy. Equality of the vote does not lead to equality of voice. We should ask Dalits who have been subjected to horrifying discrimination since the founding moment of Hindu society, the Scheduled Tribes and minorities who are ritually humiliated, women who carry ineradicable scars of violence on their bodies and minds, and children from disadvantaged families who will never know the satisfaction of leading a life that is well chosen, whether they live in a democratic society. They would turn around and ask: what on earth is democracy? This is the paramount question that should confront right-thinking Indians. What is democracy after all? Just elections that catapult conceited politicians to unthinkable power, not to better the lives of the people who voted for them, but for their own self-aggrandizement?

The latter propensity has to be controlled through the institutionalization of procedures that govern the exercise of power: division of powers, checks and balances, the rule of law, independent judiciaries, a free media and a vibrant civil society that keeps watch on the government. These features define democracy. Democracy cannot be reduced to elections alone.

## Our Prescriptive Constitution

The distinguishing character of the Indian Constitution is that it is prescriptive and it is regulatory. It is prescriptive because it institutionalizes the ideals of democracy. Left to itself, democracy can be reduced—as it can appear to have been reduced in contemporary India—to elections. And it can descend into mob rule that Greek philosophers were so wary of. Without a constitution which institutionalizes the belief that human beings deserve to be treated in certain ways, with dignity, and not to be treated in other ways, for example, subjected to custodial torture, democracy can go in any direction, or no direction except that of authoritarianism. Elections are essential for democracy, yet they are but a moment in the life of a democratic country. The essence of democracy is the right of human beings to be provided with the preconditions of a life worth living; as free and equal citizens.

As philosophers elaborate the idea of what it means to be human, the ambit of rights expands exponentially. Each right lays claims on the government. Each right adds to the concept of a life worth living. The right to live not a bare life but a life led with dignity was mandated by the Supreme Court. The right to life and liberty granted by Article 21 of the fundamental rights chapter was originally *negative* insofar as it read that 'No person shall be deprived of his life or personal liberty except according to procedure established by law'. Over time, the Supreme Court rescued Article 21 from the oblivion to which it had been relegated.

The decision of the Court in the 1950 case of *A.K. Gopalan vs the State of Madras* enlarged Article 21.[33] From a purely negative right, the right to life became a positive right obliging the government to secure the wellbeing of the people. In the case of *Maneka Gandhi vs the Union of India* (1978), the Court decided that it had the power to decide whether any procedure that affects a right was reasonable. 'The court took a great step forward by interpreting "procedure" in article 21 as "fair, reasonable, and just procedure"; thus introducing elements of procedural due process in Indian law. The courts can now insist on better procedural safeguards in cases of deprivation of personal liberty,' writes legal scholar M.P. Jain.[34]

Since 1978, Article 21 has become the repository of a

number of significant social rights thanks to the decisions of the court. The expansion of what was originally a negative right has led to the humanization of the criminal justice system. The system is now called upon to provide free legal aid to poor prisoners, and forbids torture and police brutality that is wreaked on prisoners, undertrials and accused persons. More significantly, the court has expanded the notion of mere life to a life well lived. This has in turn generated a bundle of rights.

In *Francis Coralie Mullin vs the Administrator, Union Territory of Delhi* (1981 AIR 746), the Supreme Court observed that 'the right to life includes right to live with human dignity and all that goes along with it. This includes the bare necessities of life such as adequate nutrition, clothing and shelter, facilities for reading, writing and expressing oneself in diverse forms, and freely moving about and mixing and commingling with fellow human beings. Of course, the magnitude and content of the right depends upon the economic development of the country, but it must include the right to the basic necessities of life and also the right to carry on such functions and activities as constitute the bare minimum expression of the human self'.

This formulation was further elaborated in the case of *Bandhua Mukti Morcha vs the Union of India* (1986 AIR 802). The court ruled that the right to life includes the 'right to live with human dignity, free from exploitation... [It] must include protection of the health and strength of workers, men and women, and of the tender age of children against abuse, opportunities and facilities for children to develop in a healthy manner and in conditions of freedom and dignity, educational facilities, just and humane conditions of work and maternity relief. These are the minimum conditions which must exist in order to enable a person to live with dignity and no State—neither the Central Government nor any State Government—has the right to take any action which will deprive a person of the enjoyment of these basic essentials'.

And in 1986, the court held in *Olga Tellis vs Bombay Municipal Corporation*, that the right to life includes the right to livelihood or the means of livelihood. To deprive someone of livelihood is to deprive him of the constitutional right to life: '[A]ny person who is deprived of his right to livelihood except according to just and fair procedure established by law, can challenge the deprivation as offending the right to life conferred by article 21'.[35] We see repeated references to dignity and life beyond animal existence in the radical redefinition of Article 21. The right to a meaningful life now extends from prohibitions on torture to the right to sleep.[36]

It is through a supportive Supreme Court, which interprets the Constitution creatively, that we see how democracy is much more than elections. Democracy imposes an obligation on elected governments to secure to citizens their rights. Think of what would happen if a new constitution is written by people who have little to recommend them except the fact that they are in power. We might get a constitution without its raison d'etre—the primacy of fundamental rights for all. We might get a constitution written by and for the power elite sans any of the limits that democratic constitutions set on power.

Think of what would happen if we are fated to bare life in an indifferent society that does not even try to transit to a good society. The mind boggles. Our constitution was written by people who knew what it is to stand by vulnerable sections of society without fear of consequences, arbitrary arrests, for instance. Today, Jawaharlal Nehru is openly mocked by people on the political right. They fail to recognize that Nehru spent, out of all political prisoners, the longest time in jail for the sake of his country, as a political prisoner penalized for being a freedom fighter. He could play a major role in the deliberations of the Constituent Assembly because he suffered for his people, he identified with his people and he conceptualized along with others a politically wise constitution for generations to come. His legacy will not be wiped out merely by writing over a constitution that bears his imprint. A new constitution written by majoritarians has potential for harm. This is the stark and unvarnished truth.

## Our Regulatory Constitution

The second crucial aspect of the Constitution is that it is regulatory. It regulates formulation, implementation and adjudication of policy. It guards against abuse of power and non-compliance with constitutional provisions. This is important because of what is called the paradox of democracy. We have the right to vote, and this right provides the bare bones of democracy, but we have no control over who we vote for and put into power. The paradox is that the presumptions of democracy have little relationship with outcomes. In history, tyrants have been voted into power, and once they are in power, the people who have voted for them have no control over the derailment of democracy. Further, though the majority principle is workable, it is not a moral solution to political problems. Democracy, in other words, has to be regulated by a democratic constitution.

It is therefore not surprising that liberal philosophers have been wary of demagogues and brute majorities, two factors that can cripple democratic life. They have aspired to contain both these factors to protect democracy. In the Constituent Assembly, on 25 November 1948, Dr Ambedkar counselled that we could only maintain democracy if we observed the warning that the liberal philosopher John Stuart Mill had issued to all who were interested in the maintenance of democracy. People should not 'lay their liberties at the feet of even a great man, or to trust him with powers which enable him to subvert their institutions. There is nothing wrong in being grateful to great men who have rendered life-long service to the country but there are limits to gratefulness'. He quoted the Irish patriot, Daniel O'Connell, who had said that 'no man can be grateful at the cost of his honour...and no nation can be grateful at the cost of its liberty'.[37]

The caution, continued Dr Ambedkar, is even more necessary in India: 'For in India, Bhakti or what may be called the path of devotion or hero-worship, plays a part in its politics unequalled in magnitude by the part it plays in the politics of any other country in the world. Bhakti in religion may be a road to salvation of the soul. But in politics, Bhakti or hero-worship is a sure road to degradation and to eventual dictatorship.'[38]

Dr Ambedkar's warning was prescient, for Indians have revealed a troublesome propensity to hero-worship leaders they see as strong, decisive and charismatic. This can prove favourable for democracy, and it can prove unfavourable. The

French Enlightenment thinker Voltaire had reportedly said, 'If they can make you believe absurdities, they can make you commit murder.' (I use the word reportedly advisedly because Voltaire has been credited with many quotes, some of which were rewritten by others. His actual words were: 'Truly whomsoever is able to make you absurd is able to make you unjust.'[39]) Charismatic leaders can twirl masses around their little finger, and though this skill is enviable, it is, politically speaking, dangerous.

For this precise reason, our Constitution embodies the idea of the rule of law. The rule of law protects people from arbitrary or whimsical decision-making. The French phrase 'la principe de legalite', or the principle of legality adopted during the French Revolution, translates into the rule of law and not rule by men. The famous jurist A.V. Dicey theorized that the rule of law is based upon three precepts: the supremacy of law, equality before the law and the predominance of the legal spirit. The law has to be enforced in the land and no individual can take the law into his own hands; it must be administered in a fair and just manner; and it should be enforced by an independent and impartial judiciary.

India adopted the rule of law from the Common Law system which formed the foundation of the British system of jurisprudence. Accordingly, the executive and the administration derive their power from the Constitution. This norm has been strengthened by various landmark decisions of the Supreme Court. There have been times, however, when the Supreme Court has delivered judgements against constitutionally mandated rights. This happened during the Internal Emergency

(1975–77) imposed by Prime Minister Indira Gandhi in the case of *ADM Jabalpur vs Shivkant Shukla*. The case referred to the suspension of, under Emergency provisions, Article 14, that is, the right to equality; Article 19, the right to freedom; and Article 21, the right to life. A five-judge constitution bench defended the executive by a 4-1 majority and ruled that citizens had no remedy under the law if their fundamental rights were violated. The judges who subscribed to the majority judgement were Chief Justice A.N. Ray, Justice M.H. Beg, Justice Y.V. Chandrachud and Justice P.N. Bhagwati.

The lone dissenting judgement was given by Justice H.R. Khanna. It was as analysts put it worth its 'weight in gold... The dissenting judgement continues to be the guiding light for judges even after nearly half a century and keeps reminding them about inculcating the ethos of [*sic*] constitution'.[40] Justice Khanna stated that '[e]ven in absence of Article 21 of the Constitution, the state has got no power to deprive a person of his life and liberty without the authority of law. Without such sanctity of life and liberty, the distinction between a lawless society and one governed by laws would cease to have any meaning... Rule of Law is now the accepted norm of all civilized societies'.[41]

The majority judgement in the case has been generally regarded as infamous because the issue at hand had been firmly settled by the ruling of the Supreme Court in the *Kesavananda Bharati vs the State of Kerala* case. The Supreme Court had decided then that the rule of law was part of the basic structure of the Constitution. The parliament can amend any part of the Constitution except its basic structure.[42]

The principle that has been reiterated time and again by

the highest court in the land is that the courts have the power to decide whether a law and its implementation are legally valid. That is, the court has firmly established the principle of judicial review. The whole constitutional structure is dependent upon the control of arbitrary power. In a significant sense, the power of judicial review implements the values embodied in the Preamble, the fundamental rights chapter, and in particular in Article 14, Article 21 and Article 19.

It is the grant of justiciable fundamental rights in chapter three of the Indian Constitution, the division of powers between the institutions of government, the role played by the judiciary in monitoring whether a law is in accordance with the basic structure of the Constitution and the doctrine of judicial review which constitute what has been called the regulatory aspect of the Constitution of India. This is not to suggest that power has not been abused, or that the judiciary has not been impartial and just in many cases. It is to suggest that the Constitution sets standards by which we can judge whether the executive has misused power or that the judiciary has been found wanting. Without the Constitution we would have no standards to evaluate the functioning of democracy or the lack thereof.

## The Constitution as a Social Contract and the Forging of a Political Community

Over the years, perhaps, the Constitution has begun to be taken by succeeding generations for granted; as a document that has been interpreted and reinterpreted by the Courts. Indians should recognize that the Constitution is a political and not only a legal document.

Today, once again, when many Indians have lapsed into cynicism because the project of democracy has been left unrealized, when the Constitution is violated day after day by our rulers, and hints of a new constitution replacing the current one are circulated among the people, we need to rediscover that moment of excitement and joy when India got her own constitution, to appreciate it and to fight anew for it. We have not exhausted the possibilities of the Constitution we had adopted. We need to rediscover that sense of pride that our constitution is the product of historic struggles, a democratic manifesto written amidst death and destruction.

The people of India have given fitting replies to authoritarian ruling dispensations in the past. During the Emergency in 1975, civil liberties were suspended, the courts and the bureaucracy lost autonomy, and hundreds of political opponents were jailed. In 1977, Indira Gandhi lifted the Emergency and called for elections. The Congress was spectacularly defeated, and she not only lost her constituency but also her deposit. The people of India knew that the suspension of their rights during the period had violated our democratic Constitution. This will not be possible if the Constitution is rewritten and universal adult franchise dispensed with.

Imagine what would happen if the Constitution were to be rewritten without the chapter on fundamental rights. We will be left helpless, vulnerable to state power and to the power of the dominant classes. We will live in a state of anomie and fear right out of George Orwell's *1984*. We will be subjected to laws that are neither limited by constitutional boundaries, nor by legislative procedures. Today, even if the ruling party can push through legislation without submitting bills to the committee system because it is in a majority, we know the procedure, and consequently, that the law is unjust.

We know because the Constitution has given us a benchmark to judge which law is or is not justifiable. It allows us to judge when our fundamental rights have been violated. Without the Constitution, our dreams of freedom, our aspirations to being equal to fellow citizens and our passionate desire for justice will remain unfulfilled. We will become subjects of an authoritarian state, no longer citizens of a proud republic. We need a constitution—preferably the one we currently have—simply because palpable checks on the propensity of governments to exercise uncontrollable power, which affects all of us, are necessary. It is no wonder, then, that the political theorists whose ideas gave rise to the modern state, placed necessary restrictions on its power.

In the seventeenth century, the English philosopher Thomas Hobbes (1588–1679) changed the course of political thinking. In his *Leviathan* (1651), he asked a significant question, 'Why should we obey the State?' By asking this question he performed a spectacular U-turn in political theory. Till then Aristotle's belief that the state is natural to man had ruled thinking about the relationship of human beings to the state.

For Hobbes, the natural habitat of human beings was the 'State of Nature'. In it, individuals had perfect freedom as well as a degree of equality. But they realized soon enough that without a sovereign who imposes law and order, their existence was precarious. Unless a society was politically stable, the basic instinct of man for self-preservation was in danger. So people got together and signed a metaphorical social contract that established the Leviathan/the monarch. His main obligation was to secure the right to self-preservation basic to human beings, simply because that was the reason why the institution of kingship was established. The monarch had not only to protect the lives of his subjects, but also ensure that they did not suffer from want. The concept of self-preservation included a range of goods people were entitled to. These placed limits on power. Hobbes placed far more restrictions on the power of the monarch than he has been given credit for.

The main lesson we learn from Hobbes is that the state is for its people, not the other way round. We learn from him and later social contract theorists that if the state does not provide the preconditions of wellbeing to its people, the people have the right to renege on their obligation to obey laws. In our times, modes of protest and resistance to power range from civil disobedience to the right to vote out a government.

The second lesson we learn from Hobbes is that the social contract enables people to come together in society, or in our case, in a political community. If the Indian Constitution, as a manifestation of the social contract, established a relationship between citizens and the state, it also established a relationship between citizens, simply because all of us are bound by obligation to the Constitution and to each other.

In India, the task of setting up a political community, out of hundreds of faith-based and linguistic communities, was daunting. The Partition that followed Independence had pulled people into a vortex of mind-numbing violence. The poet Firaq Gorakhpuri had famously written: '*Sar zamine-e-Hind par aqwame-e-alam ke Firaq / Kafile baste gaye / Hindostan banta gaya*'. India was created as a plural society, wrote the poet, by successive waves of migration. In 1947, sadly, the situation was reversed. The country witnessed processions of bedraggled, dispossessed people travelling from the east to the west, and from the west to the east of Punjab. As processions of dispossessed and demoralized individuals, for whom the homeland had become an arid and alien space, crossed each other, people clashed. About one million people were killed in bloody massacres; half of this number was in Punjab alone.

The Hindi poet Sachchidanand Hiranand Vatsyayan 'Agyeya' was witness to the insane bloodletting in Punjab. Overcome by regret and disbelief he wrote a series of anguished poems titled *Sharanarthi* between 12 October 1947 and 12 November of the same year. Sitting in waiting rooms, or on the benches and piles of luggage on platforms of railway stations, he scripted a testimony to the violence that was unleashed in Punjab. On 24 October 1947, he wrote: '*Aaj jaane kis hinsr dar ne / Desh ko bekhabri mein das liya / Sanskriti ki chetna murjha gayi / Mirgi ka daura pada / Ichchhashakti bujh gayi*'. (Who knows what violent dread has made the country insensible. Awareness of our common culture and of our great civilization has withered. An epileptic fit has extinguished autonomy of the will.)

After the First World War, history had once again borne witness to the nation taking precedence over solidarity. Progressive poets in newly formed Pakistan were also regretful. Ahmad Faraz, a progressive poet who had opted for Pakistan wrote: '*Ab kis ka jashn manaate ho / Us desh ka jo taqseem hua / Us desh ke geet sunaate ho / Jo toot ke hi tasleem hua*'. (What are you celebrating, a country that was created by the division of another country?) The moment of independence catapulted to the forefront mixed sentiments of joy and grief.

This formed the backdrop to the making of the Constitution. Dr Rajendra Prasad, who presided over the deliberations of the Assembly, put the matter in a nutshell. In his address to the members on 11 December 1946, he said, '[T]he Constituent Assembly is meeting at a most critical time. We all know that other constituent assemblies, whenever and wherever they met, were confronted with similar difficulties. They had also to contend with internal differences which were placed before them with great vehemence... Many of these constituent assemblies were held amidst strife and bloodshed; even their proceedings were conducted amidst quarrels and fights. Their members joined together and with courage, kindness, generosity, tolerance and regard for one another's feelings framed constitutions which were then readily accepted by the people of the countries for which they were framed.'[43] This was the specific mandate of the Constituent Assembly, to create a constitution in a spirit of 'courage, kindness, generosity, tolerance and regard for one another's feelings'.

The task was difficult. The horrors of the Partition had reduced Indians to their primal identities—Hindu, Sikh, Muslim. The miracle is that a democratic constitution was written amidst the debris of destroyed homes, workplaces, temples, gurudwaras and mosques. Yet the makers of the Constitution were aware that law alone could not consolidate a political community. Only when people were tied together by networks of mutual obligation could the traumas of the Partition be healed and people relate to each other on the basis of solidarity.

Recollect the last scene of M.S. Sathyu's 1974 film *Garm Hava*. The gifted actor Balraj Sahni plays Salim Mirza, owner of a shoe factory in Agra. The Partition hits his family the way it hit many Muslim families who had no recourse except to leave their homes and go to Pakistan, and the way it hit Hindus who had to forsake their beloved homeland in West Punjab and East Bengal and migrate to new surroundings. Sahni's entire family moves to Pakistan, and at the end he has no option except to leave his home and workplace in Agra himself. How long, he asks himself, can a man live alone? A heartbroken Sahni mounts a tonga and instructs the driver to drop him at the railway station.

This is the turning point of the film because at exactly that moment he sees a procession wending its way through the lanes of the city, carrying a red flag with the emblem of communism, the hammer and the sickle, inscribed on it. Sahni halts the tonga, straightens his cap, and joins the procession. There is a third way, he had realized, beyond the politicization of religion—solidarity with the oppressed. The Constitution, despite the fact that it was written against the background of terrible violence, showed us the third path when it adopted the concept of fraternity in the Preamble. Since fraternity is gender specific, let us use the gender-neutral term solidarity for that special obligation we have towards our fellow citizens.

Solidarity refers to the ability of people to promote the wellbeing of their fellow citizens, even if they have to pay heavily for it. For example, as we shall see later in this essay, thousands of young people across the country came together against the Citizenship Amendment Act from December 2019 to February 2020. The Act may not have affected them, but it affected, or had the potential to affect their Muslim fellow citizens. Many of these young people were put in jail, many of them were accused of being anti-national, but they stuck to the belief that we share a special relationship with our people. This special obligation inspires protest when the interests of others are adversely affected. Solidarity is a political virtue that is of intrinsic value. It allows us to move from selfishness to the recognition of our connectedness with others through webs of reciprocal obligation. It is of value because it allows citizens to speak up against power wherever and in whichever form it exists: in the hands of the capitalists, in the greasy grip of politicians, or as the disgusting caste system and patriarchy.

The construction of a political community in the post-Partition days required a great deal of intellectual and political labour and imagination. We needed leaders like Jawaharlal Nehru, but we also needed, as in the days of the freedom struggle, poets and literary figures. Some of the most inspiring poetry came from the pens of Urdu-speaking progressive poets. Elegant and evocative, Urdu was not only the language of cultivated minds but also the language spoken on the streets in large parts of the country. The tragedy of contemporary India is that it is regarded as the language of the enemy, and Urdu speakers are identified as the Other.

The devaluation of Urdu began in the decades after Independence. When the government of independent India decided to celebrate the anniversary of Mirza Ghalib in 1969, the noted poet Sahir Ludhianvi wrote with a strain of bitterness: '*Jin shahron mein goonji thi Ghalib ki nava barson / Un shahron mein aaj Urdu be-naam-o-nishan thahri / Azaadi-e-kaamil ka ailaan hua jis din / Ma'atob zabaan thahri, ghaddar zabaan thahri / Jis ahd-e-siyasat ne ye zinda zuban kuchli / Us ahd-e-siyasat ko marhoomi ka gham kyu hai / Ghalib jise kehte hain Urdu ka hi shayar tha / Urdu pe sitam dha kar, Ghalib pe karam kyu hain*'. (In cities where Ghalib's poetry used to resound, today we find no sign of Urdu. The moment independence was declared, Urdu was identified with treason. Why does this government, a government that has crushed a living language, now mourn death? Ghalib was an Urdu poet, after all. Why is he being honoured while his language has been dishonoured?)

The cynical politics of majoritarianism privileges upper-caste Sanskritic Hindi over Urdu. It forgets that revolutionary Urdu poetry which mobilized an entire generation for freedom was written by both Hindu and Muslim poets. Both loved the language, they spoke and wrote in it, and they continue to do so. Witness the passion which Urdu could arouse in the hearts of the freedom fighters. Brij Narain Chakbast (1882–1926) movingly wrote: '*Yeh Khaak-e-Hind se paide hain josh ke aasar / Himalaya se uthe jaise abr-e-daryabaar*'. (From the dust of Hindustan have arisen signs of energy and passion, the way rivers gush from the Himalayas.) Bismil Azimbadi (1901–1978) authored the marvellous poem in 1921: '*Sarfaroshi ki tamanna ab hamare dil mein hai; dekhna hai zor kitna baazu-e-katil mein hain*'. (We passionately desire to lay down our lives. Now let us see how much courage there is in the arms of the executioner.)

'Inquilab Zindabad', the phrase coined by Maulana Hasrat Mohani (1875–1951), became the rallying cry of the freedom struggle and the anthem of revolutionaries. He was demanding *azaadi-e-kaamil*, or complete independence, as early as 1921: '*Rasm-e-jafa kaamyab dekhiye kab tak rahe / Hubb-e-watan mast-e-khwab kab tak rahe / Daulat-e-Hindustan qabzah aghyar mein / Be adad o behisab dekhiye kab tak rahe*'. (Let us see how long we are oppressed, how long freedom remains but a dream, and how long the British plunder India's riches.) It was the slogan of 'Inquilab Zindabad' that Bhagat Singh, Raj Guru and Sukhdev raised as they marched to the gallows.

If revolutionaries were inspired by Chandrashekhar Azad's (1906–1931) poem, '*Dushmanon ki goliyon ka hum samna karenge / Azaad hi rahe hain, azaad hi rahenge*' (We will face the bullets of the enemy; we have been free and we will continue to be free), they were equally motivated by the poet of revolution, Josh Malihabadi (1894–1982): '*Mera naara, inquilab o inquilab o inquilab*' (My slogan is revolution).

How do we differentiate between Hindu and Muslim poetry and poets? Both passionately loved India, both strove for freedom, and both wrote amazing poetry to capture political resistance. In the process, they transformed literature and poetry. Sajjad Zaheer, a progressive writer, and one of the founders of the Progressive Writers' Association, wrote in his autobiography, *Reminiscences*: '[S]ensitive writers felt that they could not continue in the old mode... It was no longer possible for the writers to continue to live in ivory towers and remain unconcerned with the lives and thoughts of common people.' He was referring to the wave of anti-fascism, socialism and radicalization of culture, literature and poetry that swept India in the 1930s. The progressives expanded the goals of the freedom struggle to the fight against injustice and patriarchy within society. Note the contrast between progressive writers and rabid Muslim and Hindu right-wingers who remain stuck in regressive notions of there having always existed 'two nations'. The progressives taught us that society had to look outwards towards imperialism, but it also had to look inwards and focus on the many contradictions, oppressions and tyrannies within. Liberation was incomplete unless Indians liberated themselves from a class-bound, religiously bigoted and patriarchal society. They radicalized the freedom struggle. They also radicalized literature and poetry.

At the first meeting of the Progressive Writers' Association, Munshi Premchand gave the inaugural address in chaste Urdu. He told the audience that good literature can only be founded on truth, beauty, freedom and humanity. It has to reject all that inhibits human freedom and creativity, such as orthodoxy and obscurantism. 'Literature is the outward form of the artist's spiritual balance,' he said, 'and what harmony creates is never subversive. It nurtures in us the qualities of loyalty, sincerity, sympathy, justice and egalitarianism. Where these qualities exist, there is stability and life. Where they are wanting, there is division, selfishness, hatred, enmity, and death... Literature makes our life natural and free...it civilizes the self.'

Progressives showed Indians another way beyond the Hindu–Muslim binary: the domain of sensitivity and solidarity forged by the overpowering need to tackle the ills that beset the human condition. Human beings cannot be essentialized and reduced to their religious identity. They are capable of walking another path: solidarity with the oppressed, compassion for the poor and sensitivity to the sufferings of their people. This was the message of the freedom struggle and this is what the Indian Constitution prescribed for 'the people', by resolving to 'promote among [us] all fraternity'.

In a world torn apart by the violence of the Partition, however, the progressive poets had a task more immediate than that of ensuring social justice. They had to show that beyond our religious identity lay another space—that of humanity. They had now a new medium of expression through the film world, and they took up the challenge with poetic fervour and courage. Artistes like Bhisham and Balraj Sahni, Prithviraj Kapoor as well poets like Jan Nisar Akhtar, Sahir Ludhianvi and Sardar Jafri among others, spoke up against communalism, just like they did against poverty and social oppression. So did the heirs to their legacy like Raj and Shammi Kapoor and even superstars like the debonair Dev Anand.

In *Barsaat Ki Raat* (1960), Sahir Ludhianvi penned the lyrics for the famous qawwali 'Yeh Ishq hai Ishq'. The crucial words in the lyric were: '*Ishq azaad hai, Hindu na Musalman hai Ishq, aap hi dharam hai aur aap hi imaan hai Ishq*'. (Love is independent. It is neither Hindu nor Muslim; it is in itself dharma and in itself faith.) In 1961, Sahir, writing the lyrics for B.R. Chopra's *Dharamputra* (1961), asked a significant question in his poem: '*Yeh kiska lahu hai, kaun mara?*' (Whose blood is this? Who died?) The story centres around a young Shashi Kapoor (acting in his first film) who as a rabid Hindu hates Muslims. And then he discovers that he was born to Muslim parents but was adopted by a Hindu couple. The scene when he comes to terms with his identity and with the futility of hating other humans is one of the most moving scenes in the film. Rajendra Kumar, the *sutradhar* of the scene, lip-syncs the heartrending song that forms the backdrop to the realization that the politicization of religion had led to multiple tragedies. The sheer pointlessness of hating another person because of his religion, and the consequence of this hate—violence, orphaned children, women left alone to be captured and tortured by crazed mobs, burnt houses and a landscape dominated by nothing but flames as if thousands of corpses were being cremated in a gigantic crematorium—could only have been captured by Sahir's inimitable verse. He taught us that if only we were to ask the question, '*Yeh kiska lahu hai, kaun mara?*' we might realize that the blood that has been shed, often in vain, often to no purpose, belongs to our fellow citizens, to people who are a part of us, who hurt just like we do and who make us what we are. Without the 'we' there can be no I!

In the same film, a Sufi qawwali rendered before a shrine reminded us that '*Kaabe mein raho ya Kashi mein, nisbat to usiki baat se hai / Tum Ram kaho ya Rahim kaho, matlab to usiki zaat se hai*'. (Whether we stay at the Kaaba or in Kashi we are concerned with the same God. Whether we say Ram or Rahim, we refer to the same God.) Religion should not separate us from each other, it said, because all of us worship at the feet of a God who has many names and who appears to us in many forms. Religion as faith teaches us to unite with others; religion as politics divides us from each other.

When religion is politicized, we are stripped of the capacity of what the Scottish moralist philosopher Adam Smith called sympathy. 'How selfish soever a man may be supposed,' he wrote, 'there are evidently some principles in his nature, which interest him in the fortune of others, and render their happiness necessary to him, though he derives nothing from it except the pleasure of seeing it... [Emotion], like all the other original passions of human nature, is by no means confined to the virtuous and the humane... The greatest ruffian, the most hardened violator of the laws of society is not altogether without it.' This is the opening sentence of Smith's magnificently crafted *The Theory of Moral Sentiments*.[44]

Though Smith is better known for his theory of self-interested action, in this work he focused on the capacity of human beings for sympathy, an 'original passion'. Sympathy is more than fellow-feeling. People are able to feel another's pain and grieve for their calamities because they possess imagination. We can experience the torture our brother suffers on the rack through our imagination. We can forge bonds of sympathy with people we may never meet. We can share happiness and we are able to mourn together. In the political domain, sympathy provides the building block of solidarity. This is the defining feature of a democratic and humane political community, one which, for us, was outlined by our Constitution.

There is thus cause for concern today. Cast in the mould of cultural nationalism, Hindu majoritarianism leads the assault on the fellow feeling among us citizens, it calls for the erasure of all specific identities and demands the constitution of a culturally homogeneous nation. This form of nationalism—associated in history with Fascism and Nazism—is the product of particularly vicious notions of ethno-nationalism. In India, we find members of minority communities being forced on the pain of death to chant 'Jai Shri Ram'. Members of a good society do not harm another's self-respect by subjecting her or her community to discriminatory remarks, let alone expulsion or genocide. Consider how devalued we feel when we are told that our religion is of little or no value, and that our group should integrate with a dominant tradition, or assimilate. This has occurred despite the contribution of progressive poetry, the forging of solidarity, and despite secularism and minority rights that were meant to guard against these very situations. There is cause for regret.

## Chapter III

# The Discrete Charms of Secularism

Every society is troubled by social divides based on religion, or caste, or race, or ethnic identities. Democratic leaders and sane statesmen try to contain these divides so that they do not flare up as civil war. They look for commonalities that can be built upon to create a community. The Urdu poet Bashir Badr writes poignantly: '*Dushmani jam kar karo lekin ye gunjaish rahe / Jab kabhi hum dost ho jaaen to sharminda na hon*'. (Be my enemy with all the passion you command, just leave enough scope that if we, perchance, become friends, we should not be shamefaced.) Howsoever deep be the social divide, we would say in the more prosaic language of political theory, there should be some space for reconciliation.

When we think of reconciliation between hostile groups we think of Nelson Mandela. On 11 February 1990, Mandela walked out of the terrible South African prison system after twenty-seven years. The road to his home was lined with a boundless sea of people, cheering, holding flags and banners, clapping, dancing and laughing. Addressing enthusiastic crowds, he said, 'Friends, comrades and fellow South Africans, I greet you all in the name of peace, democracy and freedom for all!' Freedom for all was to become his mantra for a democratic and inclusive country.

At a press conference held after his release, Mandela gave us the answer to the question that troubles all societies. His formulation resonated with generosity, forethought and cool, sane politics. He did not want the white community to be driven away; this would devastate the country. Whites, he said, were fellow South Africans and anyone who abandoned apartheid had a place in a democratic South Africa. Black Africans had to learn to live with their erstwhile oppressors. Whites had to give up the dream, espoused by many, that they be given a separate state. Mandela was prescient. Secession or partition of territory is a relatively easy option. What is more difficult is to encourage people to give up violence and to learn to live together.

The question that occupied him was similar to the one India had to confront since at least the beginning of the twentieth century. How do people belonging to different religious faiths manage to live together? And then came Partition, which left ineradicable scars in the minds of Indians and Pakistanis. The Punjabi poet and writer Amrita Pritam captured the enormity of violence when in her poem 'Ajj Aakhaan Waris Shah Nu' she implored the eighteenth-century Sufi poet of the Chishti order, and the author of the epic poem, *Heer Ranjha*, Waris Shah, to rise from his grave and testify to the bloodshed of the Partition, and the fate of the women.

You wept when one of the daughters of Punjab, Heer, died

of grief, she wrote. Today, I ask Waris Shah, rise from your grave and look at the fate of the thousands of daughters of Punjab. The pastures are strewn with corpses, and the Chenab runs red with blood. This has happened in the same Punjab whose riches were once spoken of in admiring terms.

Of course, there were sane voices on both sides, and there were leaders and poets, writers and playwrights who reminded people that they had the same roots, and that two cultures remain part of their blood. To cite Kanvil Ziai, the nom de plume of Hardayal S. Dutta (1927–2011): '*Hamara khoon ka rishta hai sarhadon ka nahi / Hamare khoon men Ganga bhi, Chanab bhi hai*'. (Our relationship is based not on borders but on a common bloodline; in our blood runs both the Ganga and the Chenab.) Yet the state of the country, divided as it was on the grounds of religion, was precarious. It was clear that the newly independent state could not afford to give precedence to the majority religion. It was also clear that the sections of the Muslim community that had opted not to go to Pakistan but stay behind in their homeland must be made to feel safe and protected. India was host to Sikhs, Parsis, Buddhists, Jains, Christians and animists as well. The idea was to make sure that none should feel disadvantaged in a country in which Hindus were a majority.

## Secularism and Minority Rights

The precedents for tolerance, pluralism and secularism had been laid in the 1920s. M.K. Gandhi, who emerged as an outstanding leader of the Indian National Congress in that decade, had an unusual ability to touch hearts and harness political imaginations in the cause of freedom. Under his leadership, the scale of the struggle expanded exponentially. However, at the same time, in the first half of the twentieth century, India also witnessed the unleashing of rabid communal violence and a hardening of political/national positions.[45]

The birth of a number of fundamentalist organizations in the 1910s and 1920s had transformed religion as faith into religion as power politics. The process intensified as the Muslim League began to hint at a separate state. Unlike the experience of Europe during the Enlightenment, religion had not retreated into the private sphere. It had entered the public sphere with competitive mobilization around it as the base of a future nation-state. The future was thus bound to be turbulent. Faith heals, but the politics of religion divides communities.

Historians tell us that the colonial government fomented the religious divide by interpreting every clash as a communal riot, by the introduction of the Census that made clear demographic majorities and minorities, and by the introduction of separate electorates. This formed the background to constitution-making in India. The leaders of the freedom struggle had to find creative solutions to this problem.

In 1928, when the All Parties Conference set out to create a draft constitution, leaders appealed to the Muslim League to join the effort. The League agreed to join only if the constitutional draft provided for separate electorates. The leaders of the All Parties Conference refused to do so. A way out was found in the commitment to minority rights. The first assurance was coded in clause XI of the section on fundamental rights of the

Motilal Nehru Draft. It stated that no religion would be given the status of a state religion for the Commonwealth of India, or for any province. Nor shall the state, the document stated, either directly or indirectly endow any religion, give any preference, or impose any disability on account of religious beliefs and status. The state was, in sum, enjoined not to interfere in religion.

But in an attempt to protect minority religions from the onslaught of the majority, secularism came to acquire a completely different hue than it had taken on in the West. The principle of the separation of religion and politics was the approach European countries had adopted. In India, however, both politics and policy recognized the salience of religious identity in the public sphere.

The twelfth clause protected minorities from discrimination. Non-discrimination is the weaker form of equality. No person shall be obliged to attend, it stated, religious instructions in schools receiving state aid or public money. According to clause XIII of the Draft, no person shall by reason of his religion caste or creed, be prejudiced in any way with regard to public employment, office of power, honours or the exercise of any trade and calling. Subsequent clauses guaranteed non-discrimination in the use of public roads, public wells and places of public resort. All citizens were granted equal rights. The right to equality was backed by minority rights.

In 1930, Pandit Jawaharlal Nehru authored a perceptive note on the issue in *Young India*. 'The history of India and Europe', he wrote, 'has demonstrated that there can be no stable equilibrium in any country if attempts are made to crush minorities or force them to conform to the ways of the majority.

There is no surer method of rousing the resentment of the minority and keeping it apart from the mainstream than to make it feel that it has not got the freedom to stick to its own ways... [W]e in India must make it clear to all that our policy is based on granting this freedom to the minorities and that under no circumstances will any coercion or repression of them be tolerated... Indeed we should go further and state that it will be the business of the state to give favoured treatment to minority and backward communities.'[46]

This commitment was reiterated in 1931 after savage Hindu–Muslim riots in Kanpur. A miasma of devastation and gloom hung over the city as the clashes left 400 dead, parts of the city destroyed, mosques and temples damaged and houses burnt. In the aftermath of the Kanpur riots, the Indian National Congress established an enquiry commission to explore the reasons for the violence. A small committee of prominent Congressmen, Purshottam Das Tandon, Khwaja Abdul Majid, T.A.K. Sherwani, Zaraful Mulk, Pandit Sunderlal and Bhagwan Das, authored a report that has been described as an elaborate, contemporary nationalist statement on the history of Hindu–Muslim relations in India.[47] Communal riots are an outcome, the report concluded, of certain historical and social processes that have been sparked off by colonial rule. The argument overturned the assumption, widely disseminated by the colonial government, that Hindu–Muslim enmity was endemic to India. The maintenance of peace, on the latter grounds, required the presence of British rule.

Historians tell us that the pejorative term 'communal' was practically invented by the colonial government. The Indian

National Congress uncritically accepted the term 'communal', but held that it was the British policy of divide and rule that was responsible for violence, loss of lives and destruction in communal riots. The official Congress position was that India was home to both Hindus and Muslims, and that it was possible to put an end to the conflict only if minorities were assured that their rights to religion and culture would be given full protection in an independent India.

Three features distinguished the official position of the Congress on communal violence and minority rights. One, the leaders accepted that the Hindu majority was as guilty of communal sentiments and violence as the Muslim minority. Two, the state had to be neutral towards all religions. Three, group rights for minorities were not only an essential precondition for individual rights, but important in themselves. In other words, religion was seen as a significant good to which all people had a right. And further, in a society where the Hindu community had the advantage of numbers, minorities had to be protected against Hindu majoritarianism.

In the shadow of the 1931 Kanpur riots, the Congress drafted the Karachi Resolution on Fundamental Rights. The declaration emphasized the right to religion and the freedom to profess and practise any religion. A new addition to the list of minority rights was the right to cultural autonomy, and equal access to educational facilities. On 31 March 1931, Gandhi, moving the resolution on fundamental rights in the open session of the Congress at Karachi, spoke on the issue. '[T]hough I am sure that Islamic and Aryan cultures are not mutually exclusive and fundamentally different,' he said, 'I must recognize that Mussalmans look upon Islamic culture as distinctive from Aryan. Let us therefore cultivate tolerance.'[48] 'Religious neutrality is another important provision,' he continued. 'Swaraj will favour Hinduism no more than Islam, nor Islam more than Hinduism... Let us from now on,' he concluded, 'adopt the principle of state neutrality in our daily affairs.'[49]

In November 1944, a non-party conference appointed a thirty-member committee of distinguished Indians, headed by Tej Bahadur Sapru, to examine and resolve issues thrown up by the minority question, particularly the impasse between the Indian National Congress and the Muslim League on the constitutional future of India. The report of the committee, which was made public in 1945, recommended full religious tolerance, non-interference in religious beliefs, practices and institutions, and protection of the language and culture of all communities.

## Secularism in the Constituent Assembly

Though Congress leaders often used the term secularism in the pre-Independence period, oddly enough the concept was never spelt out or elaborated as a principle of state policy. Nor did it form part of the Preamble to the Constitution till 1976, when it was added to it by the 42nd Amendment. But the spirit of secularism was present throughout the debates in the Constituent Assembly. For instance, most members agreed that the Preamble to the Constitution should not contain any reference to God. On 17 October 1949, during discussions on the wording of the Preamble, H.V. Kamath moved an amendment that the Preamble should begin with the phrase 'In the name of God'. Similar amendments were moved by Shibban Lal Saxena and Pandit Madan Mohan Malaviya. Other members objected, and a majority of the members expressed their conviction that religion was a matter of individual choice and not the signpost of a collective.[50] For Pandit Hriday Nath Kunzru (United Provinces, General), 'it [wa]s a matter of the deepest regret that a matter that concerns our innermost and most sacred feelings should have been brought into the arena of discussion. It would have been far more consistent with our belief in the highest truths and our determination to adhere firmly to them that we should not seek to impose our own belief on others... We invoke the name of God, but I make bold to say that while we do so, we are showing a narrow, sectarian spirit, which is contrary to the spirit of the Constitution'.[51] The amendment moved by Mr Kamath was defeated.

It is thus quite puzzling that despite copious references to secularism, no one seemed to be quite sure what the concept stood for. On 15 November 1948, K.T. Shah (Bihar, General) moved an amendment to Article 1. The amendment held that clause 1 of Article 1, will read as follows: 'India shall be a Secular, Federal, Socialist Union of States.' '[W]e have been told,' he stated, 'time and again, from every platform, that ours is a secular State. If that is true, if that holds good, I do not see why the term could not be added or inserted in the constitution itself, once again, to guard against any possibility of misunderstanding or misapprehension.'

Shah argued that every constitution reflects the spirit and the tensions of its age. The pre-Independence period was scarred by communal riots, and Independence was accompanied by its unhappy twin—the Partition of India. To avoid a repetition of these experiences, the character and nature of the state, which was being constituted by the Assembly, should assure all citizens that relations between citizens, the relation of the citizen to the state, and the relationship of the states inter se would not be influenced by any consideration which might result in injustice or inequality.[52]

Dr Ambedkar (Bombay, General) in a longish reply to this observation focused on the implications of the term socialist, but completely ignored the suggestion that secularism should be institutionalized as the governing principle of democracy. The amendment was rejected on the plea that 'the Constitution...is merely a mechanism for the purpose of regulating the work of the various organs of the State... The policy of the State, how the Society should be organized in its social and economic side are matters which must be decided by the people themselves according to time and circumstances'.[53] In the process, the exact meaning of secularism remained undetermined even though the concept was mentioned in the context of the role of religion in political and social life.

For example, on 23 November 1948, K.M. Munshi emphasized that religion must be restricted to spheres which legitimately appertain to religion. The rest of life must be regulated, unified and modified in order to build a strong and consolidated nation.[54] On 2 December 1948, Dr Ambedkar asked for strict control over religion.[55] 'The religious conceptions in this country are so vast that they cover every aspect of life,' he said, 'from birth to death... [W]e ought to strive to limit the definition of religion in such a manner that we shall not extend beyond beliefs and such rituals as may be connected with ceremonials.'

'I do not see,' continued Dr Ambedkar, 'why religion should be given this vast, expansive jurisdiction as to cover the whole of life and to prevent the legislature from encroaching upon that field. After all what are we having this liberty for? We are having this liberty to reform our social system, which is so full of inequalities, discrimination and other things that conflict with our fundamental rights.'

At the same time, the hold of religion on social life had to be loosened and its range circumscribed in the interests of justice and equality. Consequently, a host of laws instituted social reform in Hindu law. Significantly, minorities were assured that their identities would not be at risk in a society dominated by Hindus. Pandit Nehru had been unequivocal in stating, both inside and outside the Assembly, that whatever the shape of things might be in Pakistan, India would pursue with great vigour efforts to form a secular state, in which everybody could walk with her head held high. India, he declared, 'was a secular nation which guarantees equality of citizenship to people of all religions'.[56]

Therefore, we have Article 14, which guarantees equality before the law and equal protection of the laws, and Article 15(1), which states that the state shall not discriminate against any citizen on grounds only of religion, race, caste, sex, place of birth, or any of them. Article 16(2) guarantees that there shall be no discrimination on the grounds of religion and caste in employment or appointment of any official under the state. Article 25(1) grants freedom of religion subject to public morality and health.

But what precisely is secularism?

On 24 January 1948, Prime Minister Jawaharlal Nehru clarified the notion of secularism in a convocation address to the Aligarh Muslim University. In the middle of a fluid situation caused by the Partition, he said, 'All of us have to be clear about our basic allegiance to certain ideas. Do we believe in a national state which includes people of all religions and shades of opinion and is essentially secular as a state, or do we believe in the religious, theocratic conception of a state that considers other people as beyond the pale? ... [T]he idea of a theocratic state was given up some centuries ago and it has no place in the mind of a modern man. And yet the question has to be put in India today, for many of us have tried to jump back to a past age... Whatever confusion the present may contain, in the future India will be a land, as in the past, of many faiths equally honoured and respected, but of one national outlook, not, I hope, a narrow nationalism living in its own shell, but rather [a] tolerant, creative nationalism...'[57]

The first principle of secularism is the freedom of every community to practise its religion. The second principle of secularism is that religion is recognized as a constituent of social and thus political relations. Nehru clarified this when he said, 'We call our State a secular one. The word "secular" perhaps is not a very happy one. And yet, for want of a better, we have used it. What exactly does it mean? It does not obviously mean a state where religion as such is discouraged. It means freedom of religion and conscience, including freedom for those who may have no religion.'[58]

Strictly speaking, we do not need to proclaim secularism in order to grant religious freedom. This freedom can emerge from, and form part of, Article 19, guaranteeing the fundamental right to liberty that is assured to every citizen. But a secular state cannot stop at granting the right to religious freedom. The principle of secularism goes further and establishes equality between all religious groups. Certainly, the generic right to equality, granted by Article 14 of the chapter on fundamental rights, can protect equality among religious communities. But if we were to stop at this, secularism would be rendered unnecessary; it could well be collapsed into democracy.

Secularism extends beyond equality and freedom in two ways. As a companion concept of democracy, secularism extends individual rights to equality *to* religious communities while guaranteeing equality *between* them. Two, the state is not aligned to any religion. Or secularism, we can say, promises that the state would neither align itself with any one religion—especially the majority religion—nor pursue any religious tasks of its own, and further, that it will *ensure that religious minorities are treated equally by the state.* These commitments establish the credentials of a secular state.

The equality of all religions and the distancing of the state from all religious groups were specifically meant to assure the minorities that they had a legitimate place as citizens in the country, and that they would not be discriminated against. Correspondingly, secularism established that the majority group could not be privileged in any manner. The creed simply discouraged any pretension that a majority had any right to stamp the body politic with its ethos. It is this political task that is allotted to secularism in a plural society like ours, and it is the significance of this political task that is overlooked by critics of secularism in India.

The Congress, as we have seen, was committed to the protection of minority culture and religion since 1928. The Sub-Committee on Minorities within the Constituent Assembly, headed by H.C. Mookherjee, had in its report of 27 July 1947 recommended that seats should be reserved under joint electorates. Two, minority interests should be protected through a convention under a Schedule to the Constitution. Three, reservations for minorities should be provided in the public services but these should be balanced against merit and efficiency. Four, independent officers should be appointed to report to the legislatures on the working of safeguards.[59]

The Advisory Committee on Fundamental Rights accepted these proposals in its report on minority rights in August 1947. On 27 and 28 August, the Constituent Assembly adopted the report in its entirety, and in February 1948, these provisions were incorporated into the draft constitution in Part XIV. However, some members of the Advisory Committee—Tajamul Hussain and H.C. Mookherjee—reopened the issue of political rights in a meeting of the Committee on 30 December 1948 in light of the Partition. Reserved seats were considered undesirable, because they conflicted with secularism. The resolution to delete these provisions moved by Mookherjee was accepted by the Advisory Committee, and this was communicated to the Constituent Assembly by Sardar Patel on 11 May 1949. Pandit Nehru supported the withdrawal of reservations. 'The only way to proceed about it...is to remove every barrier which separates [the majority and the minority] in the political domain so that they may develop and we may all work together'.[60]

But the Constituent Assembly did honour the historical commitment to the educational and the cultural rights of minorities. Article 29(1) of the fundamental rights chapter establishes that 'any section of the citizens residing in the territory of India or any part thereof, having a distinct language, script or culture of its own shall have the right to conserve the same'. Article 30 guarantees that all religious and linguistic minorities are given the right to establish and administer educational institutions of their choice. Recognizing that in a society dominated by one religion, i.e. Hinduism, minorities can be at risk, every community, whether it is a minority or majority, has the right to preserve its culture vide Article 29. The right is, however, an individual right, and no provision is made for the preservation of a culture or religion that might be under threat.[61]

## Interpretations by the Judiciary: Triumphs and Pitfalls

Given that secularism had not been defined in the Constitution and did not form part of the Preamble till the 1970s, given that the meaning Nehru allotted to the concept was not codified in law, and above all, given that the concept is neither self-evident nor self-explanatory, the task of defining and elaborating the concept of secularism has fallen upon the shoulders of the Supreme Court. On 27 October 2016, amidst an acrimonious legal debate on curbing the role of religion in electioneering, the Supreme Court rhetorically asked whether secularism meant the complete separation of religion from politics. The then Chief Justice Thakur, Justices Madan B. Lokur, S.A. Bobde, Adarsh K. Goel, U.U. Lalit, D.Y. Chandrachud and L.N. Rao concluded that secularism does not mean that the state should stay aloof from religion, but that it should give equal treatment to every religion. Religion and caste are vital aspects of our polity and it is not possible to completely separate them from politics, they argued.[62]

The Supreme Court was reiterating what an earlier court had ruled in the case of *S.R. Bommai vs the Union of India*. Within general considerations of the federal principles, the complex of judgements in the *Bommai* case established both the meaning and the significance of secularism in India.

In 1994, the Supreme Court had to decide whether, in the aftermath of the destruction of the Babri mosque in 1992, the dismissal of three state governments by the central government and the imposition of President's Rule, was justified. The three states were Madhya Pradesh, Rajasthan and Himachal Pradesh. It was alleged that two of the three chief ministers belonged to the Rashtriya Swayamsevak Sangh, and that the three states had sent *kar sevaks* (volunteers) to Ayodhya to participate in the bringing down of the mosque. The issue before the Court was that of federalism and the right of the central government to dismiss state governments under Article 356 of the Constitution. The Court, in the process of delivering the judgement, elaborated the principle of secularism. The issue came up because it was alleged by the central government that the sending of kar sevaks to Ayodhya violated the principle of secularism which is part of the basic structure of the Constitution.

The Court had previously declared, in the 1973 case of *Kesavananda Bharti vs the State of Kerala*, that principles that formed the 'basic structure' of the Constitution were not subject to amendment by any legislative authority. And so, what remained to be established here was whether secularism was part of that basic structure.

The Supreme Court upheld the assertion that secularism is part of the basic structure of the Constitution. But what, asked Ram Jethmalani, one of the counsel for the petitioners, *is* secularism? It is a vague, ill-defined concept, a vacuous word, a phantom concept that will not bear the weight of the actions undertaken in its name.[63]

The Supreme Court thereon proceeded to define secularism in judgements delivered by different justices. The set of judgements in the *Bommai* case are lengthy and complex but we can isolate the following themes that are of interest to the argument at hand. One, secularism is part of the basic structure of the Constitution and therefore cannot be violated or amended. Two, secularism is derived from the Hindu *principle* of tolerance, or '*sarva dharma sambhaav*'. It thereby ensures the equality of religions. The state is enjoined to accord equal treatment to all religions and religious sects and denominations. Three, the court reiterated Nehru's opinion that no religion should be at risk in a secular India, because the government will not be aligned to religion. Four, there is an essential connection between secularism and democracy. The concept of the secular state is essential for the working of democracy, and the realization of social and economic needs that are essential for material and moral prosperity and political justice.[64]

As will be seen, the concept continues to be defined on the terrain of an overriding principle: sarva dharma sambhaav. This gives reason for some perplexity. Should a multi-religious society be governed by principles that are overtly Hindu and that are not subscribed to by other religious communities? Political theorist Bhikhu Parekh has outlined a critique of this interpretation. Hindu pluralism is hierarchically structured but is also the basis of a new hierarchy, writes Parekh. Hindus are convinced that no religion exhausts the truth. It follows that other religions that claim perfection are flawed. The consequence is that, for Hindus, who claim superiority, other religions are to be *tolerated*, never accepted as equals.[65] The problem is that Islam and Christianity do not accept that all beliefs lead the way to the divine, and Buddhism and Jainism do not subscribe to any notion of God. To equate secularism with the principle of sarva dharma sambhaav lands us firmly into the domain of majoritarian notions of what secularism means.

Whereas on the one hand the judiciary defined secularism, on the other, it clarified the nature of religion. In a sense, the Supreme Court has carried on the colonial project of defining and conceptualizing religion. It has also carried on the nationalist project of reforming Hinduism. Consider the 'Hindutva Judgement', a series of seven rulings of the Supreme Court in December 1995. The issue at hand was the Representation of People Act, 1951, which establishes the meaning of corrupt practices during an election. The use of money, and an appeal for votes by invoking religious animosity can subject candidates to serious legal penalties, including reversal of election wins. This case involved corruption charges against Ramesh Yeshwant

Prabhoo, the mayor of Bombay, and his election agent, Bal Thackeray. They were accused of promoting enmity on religious grounds.

Chief Justice J.S. Verma of the Supreme Court upheld the relevant sections of the RPA. Justice Verma ruled that under the guise of protecting one's own religion, culture or creed, groups and individuals cannot lead personal attacks on others, or whip up low instincts and fear among groups to secure electoral victories. Both the appellants were held guilty of corrupt practice. At the same time, the three-judge bench held that appeals for votes in the name of Hindutva are a legitimate course of action.

In the process, the Supreme Court engaged in a long disquisition on the nature of Hindutva, which it saw as synonymous with Hinduism. The bench thus obscured the distinction between religion as faith and politicized religion as an ideology of the religious right. The Court proceeded to define Hinduism as a diverse set of practices rather than a coherent religion. Drawing upon scholarly works, the court suggested that organized religion is characterized by one holy book, a church and one prophet. Hinduism is different; it is a way of life as Dr Sarvepalli Radhakrishnan had theorized in his scholarly works. Clearly, the shadow of Orientalism loomed large upon the ruling of the court.

The judgement raises several troublesome issues. For example, if candidates seeking votes appeal to Hinduism *as a religion*, the practice falls within the ambit of corrupt practices. But if they appeal to Hinduism/Hindutva *as a way of life*, this cannot be considered a corrupt practice. The onus is upon candidates; they have to establish the specific sort of Hinduism that has been used to appeal for votes.[66] This definition of Hinduism, consequently, remains vague and contested.

It is thus a pity that the Constituent Assembly did not define secularism and it has been left to the Court to expound on the theme and establish the relationship of religion to public and political life. Resultantly, the concept has been widened out alarmingly and made to take on various tasks it is not capable of. So let us clarify some basic facts about secularism.

Secularism is not a robust concept like democracy or justice. The specific meaning given to it, that of equality between religions, accepts that religion plays an important role in the public sphere. But the coexistence of religious identity and democratic politics is not easy. Religion gives to believers 'thick' or comprehensive conceptions of the good that help them to make sense of the world, order their lives and relate to others. This is the basis of religious assertions in the public sphere. The concept of secularism is, in comparison, 'thin', insofar as it merely establishes procedures that indicate what the place of religion in the public domain is, and what the relationship between different groups should be. Secularism contributes to normative constitutional principles, but it is not a stand-alone concept; it is part of the democratic imaginary. If Article 14 establishes equality between citizens, secularism establishes equality between religious groups.

Per se, therefore, it has little to do with inequality or gender injustice within religious groups. These fall within the provenance of democracy. Democratic principles should regulate relationships within a religious group. Secularism is a weak form of equality. More specifically, it establishes the principle of non-discrimination *between* religious groups. However, if a group is in a numerical minority and is vulnerable to the threats of the majority, its culture and educational rights are protected by Articles 29 and 30, commonly known as minority rights. More significantly, secularism elaborates the democratic principle that the state is not aligned to one group, howsoever dominant it may be. In the social world, secularism can succeed in achieving its objectives only if people comprehend the significance of equality both for themselves and their relationship with fellow citizens. In the political world, members of the majority group have no special claim upon power. In a democracy, minority groups should not be discriminated against even though they are demographically lesser than others.

Though secularism has been presented as the binary opposite of religion, or as in India, communalism, it is the binary opposite of theocracy, which concentrates religious and political power in one set of hands. Religion as politics is not religion as faith. Politics and religion address different facets of the human experience. The challenge to secularism does not emanate from the leaders of personal faith, but from politicized groups that act in the name of their religious community.

The basic principle of democracy is that every religious denomination in a multi-religious society like India deserves equal respect. Judicial interpretations have reinforced this idea of equality. This is particularly important for India where religion has been politicized and yoked to the pursuit of political power—with devastating consequences. Denial of secularism raises issues about the rights and privileges of citizenship, and throws into sharp relief the intersections between religion and other concerns such as a lack of voice of the minorities, and the recognition of the distinctiveness of groups. To challenge secularism is therefore to challenge democracy as we know it.

The continuing debate on secularism, even though the environment is not conducive to the idea, and although secularism is sometimes dismissed as 'sickularism', proves the relevance of the concept. We should admire the makers of the Constitution. They left room for creative interpretations of the foundational principles of Indian democracy even as they reiterated the basic ideas they were committed to.

An instance of this wisdom is illustrated by the following incident. On 1 May 1947, Mahavir Tyagi, the Congress member from the United Provinces suggested that consideration of minority rights should be postponed. 'If there is to be a partition, we must know what is happening to the minorities on the other side, in the other units.'[67] Dr Ambedkar, the Chairman of the Drafting Committee, replied resolutely that the rights of minorities are absolute rights, that they should not be held hostage to the policies of another country or its minorities.

Let us accept that in a multi-religious society, we need to secularize secularism, by removing it from the domain of religiosity, and ground it in Article 14 that grants the right to equality. This was the original meaning of secularism conceptualized by the makers of the Constitution.

## Chapter IV

# Redistribution and the Constitution

'*Garibi / Ek khuli hui kitab / Jo har samajdhar / Aur murkh ke haath mein di gayi hai / Kuch use padhte hain / Kuch uske chitr dekh / Ulat-pulat rakh dete hai / Neeche showcase ke*'. Poverty, writes the 'angry young man' of Hindi poetry, Sudama Pandey 'Dhoomil', is an open book that has been handed over to the wise and the fools alike. Some read it, others look at the photographs and then place it higgledy-piggledy below the bookcase. The poet in effect tells us that Indians are quite indifferent to the sorry spectacle of misery that surrounds us.

The poet makes a point that is worrying. January 2023 brought news that should stagger every right-thinking Indian. The Oxfam Inequality Report showed that 5 per cent of Indians own 60 per cent of the country's wealth, whereas the bottom 50 per cent of the population owns only 3 per cent. The marginalized continue to suffer in a system which ensures the 'survival of the richest'. Considering that the Constitution promises in the Preamble equality and justice to every citizen, we are entitled to ask: what has gone wrong with our democracy? Why are people indifferent to poverty that stalks the heels of millions of their fellow citizens? Why has this happened despite a strong history of protest at inequalities and oppressions since the early twentieth century—workers' strikes, peasant revolts and a robust literary and poetic tradition that aroused political awareness about the country as it is and as it should be?

Consider the history of political liberalism in India, a liberalism that, staying away from identity politics, concentrated on extracting civil liberties, political rights and social goods for the population from the colonial regime. Though 'liberalism' is more of a family of concepts ranging from the right to private property and limited government (at the time of John Locke), to the right to redistributive justice (in the work of John Rawls), to minority rights (in Will Kymlicka), let us look at what precisely was considered liberal in India at the turn of the twentieth century.

India was racked by plague at the end of the nineteenth century in the Bombay Presidency and a devastating famine in 1899. Leading intellectuals and political figures came to the conclusion that end of the British Raj was near. Allan Octavian Hume, the founder of the Indian National Congress, saw only one possible trajectory for India—oceans of blood.[68] Foremost among the critics of the Raj was a prominent liberal scholar and parliamentarian, Dadabhai Naoroji (1825–1917). Naoroji was an outstanding scholar who authored a number of works criticizing the indifference of the colonial government to social wellbeing. Focusing on the 'drain of wealth' from India to England, Naoroji's meticulous research revealed the multiple ways in which British colonial rule was responsible for famines that took millions of lives. Among his programme for social wellbeing was compulsory and free primary education, free higher education and the Indianization of the bureaucracy. More Indians in the civil service, he believed, might just make the government more responsive to the ills that beset the Indian people.

Naoroji's biographer, Dinyar Patel, calls him the pioneer of Indian nationalism.[69] He made history when he located the concept of Swaraj as the core of the political agenda at a massive public meeting held by the Indian National Congress in 1906. Lambasting the British government for its inattention to illbeing in the country, he suggested that matters could only be improved when the country was given the right to self-government, or Swaraj.

Along with Naoroji, early Congress liberals, Pherozeshah Mehta (1845–1915), Surendranath Bannerjee (1848–1925) and G.K. Gokhale (1866–1915), criticized the British government for its failure to give to Indians the same rights as it gave its own citizens. They also questioned its failure to uphold its historic role as the vehicle of liberalism and maker of liberal institutions such as the rule of law, and constitutionalism. The common feature of Indian liberalism, writes historian C.A. Bayly, 'was a desire to re-empower India's people with personal freedom in the face of the despotic government of foreigners'.[70] It follows that our leaders saw as the precondition of individual freedom a measure of independence from imperial rule. The collective right to freedom from imperialism was a necessary precondition to the individual Indian's right not to be poor, or hungry, or ill.

It took Indian liberals three decades from the last years of the nineteenth century—when they were content with demanding Dominion Status—to arrive at a radical position in 1929, when the Indian National Congress placed the demand of Purna Swaraj, total independence, at the high table of politics.

The unwavering focus on autonomy from alien rule distinguished Indian liberalism from the British tradition. More significantly, whereas British liberals believed in a *laissez faire* state right up to the Second World War, and whereas they upheld the institution of private property, Indians believed that the state had to intervene in industry and agriculture to protect workers and farmers from the depredations of colonial capitalism.

For example, M.G. Ranade (1842–1901) argued that private property and freedom of contract and competition, which were the key assumptions of classical political economy, were not enough to secure the wellbeing of the peasants and workers. The state had to intervene to take care of essential needs, and to invest in state sponsored industrialization, protection of local industry, and the fixing of rents, tenures and rates of interest.[71]

There was a perceptible shift by the 1920s as the political discourse expanded the idea of rights from civil and political to an emphasis on social rights. The Commonwealth of India Bill (1925), discussed in the chapter on the making of the Constitution, asserted the right to free primary education. Given the context of the times it is not surprising that the Bill proposed a restricted franchise, confined to the educated, the employed and the tax-payer. Political scientist Niraja Jayal records Gandhi's response to the proposal. He objected to the fact that there was no provision for labour in the franchise. 'My formula is, no labour, no vote, hence the spinning franchise.'[72]

The principle of universal adult franchise was coded in 1928, when the Motilal Nehru Draft Constitution recognized the significance of an integrated system of rights that reached across traditional divides in rights talk. In his report to the All Parties Conference, Pandit Motilal Nehru stated: 'We cannot believe that a future responsible government can ignore the claims of mass education, or the uplift of the submerged classes, or the social or economic reconstruction of village life in India.'[73] Accordingly, primacy was given to the right to free elementary education without distinction of caste or creed in any educational institution maintained or aided by the state. Such a right, stated the report, shall be enforceable as soon as a competent authority establishes an educational system.

The report obliged a future parliament to make suitable laws for the maintenance of health and fitness for work for all citizens, for securing a living wage for all workers, for the protection of motherhood and the welfare of children, and also protection from the economic consequences of old age, infirmity and unemployment. It granted the right of association and the right to form unions in order to maintain and improve labour relations and economic conditions. The All Parties Conference, which considered the report in the last week of August 1928, suggested the addition of a clause directing a future parliament to make laws ensuring fair rent, as well as fixity and permanence of tenure for agricultural tenants.[74] This clause was added to the list of social rights enumerated in the supplementary report issued by an expanded committee in September 1928.[75]

The importance of social rights was reiterated in the Resolution on Fundamental Rights and Economic and Social Change adopted by the Congress session in Karachi in March 1931, in the aftermath of the Kanpur communal riot. The resolution contained a declaration of rights, and publicly proclaimed a commitment to redistribution: in order 'to end the exploitation of the masses, political freedom must include the real economic freedom of the starving millions'. The state was expected to safeguard the interests of industrial workers, ensure a living wage, healthy conditions of work, limited hours of labour, and protection from the economic consequences of old age, sickness and unemployment. Women and children were given protection. The state would own or control key industries and services, mineral resources, railways, waterways, shipping and other means of public transport. Also mandated was the reform of land tenure, rent and revenue.

In the Constituent Assembly, the discussion around the Objectives Resolution generated the legitimate expectation that social rights would form an intrinsic part of the fundamental rights chapter. These expectations were disproved when the Advisory Committee on Fundamental Rights (appointed by a resolution of the Assembly on 24 January 1947) concluded that rights should be divided into two parts—rights of citizens and directive principles for the government.

The decision is inexplicable. Every factor to facilitate the codification of social rights as constitutional entitlements was in place: historical legacies, constitutional drafts, and political commitments, as well as demands for redistributive justice from some very radical workers' and peasants' agitations in the 1940s.

The eminent historian Sumit Sarkar, who has edited a massive volume of documents on the movement for Independence in the year 1946 under the *Towards Freedom* project, tells us that labour movements under predominantly Communist or Left leadership remained extremely formidable throughout much of 1946 (the immediate period before the meeting of the Constituent Assembly), particularly from March to September. The movements acquired in some sectors an unprecedented countrywide sweep. Particularly striking was the advance in white-collar militancy and organizations, for example, the postal strike of July 1946. Peasant unrest mounted in some regions and the country witnessed the beginning of the Tebhaga movement in Bengal. The movement arose when peasants demanded two-thirds share of the product. These movements were not directly anti-British,[76] writes Sarkar. Arguably, they fed into an expanded notion of freedom from imperial rule, as well as freedom from constraints posed by landlords and industrialists. The demand of the hour was an integrated list of political, civil and social rights.

But when the time came to include the right to wellbeing in the Constitution, social rights were consigned to the non-justiciable section of Directive Principles. We can with the benefit of hindsight assume that one of the reasons for the enduring poverty in India is that social rights—to an income, shelter, health and education—were not a part of the fundamental rights chapter of the Constitution. A right lays a pressing claim upon the state to deliver the good the right is a right to. Directive principles are just guidelines.

## Social Rights: The Creative Phase

A drive to upgrade *directive principles* to *rights* gained steam in the first decade of the twenty-first century. In the period 2004–14, social legislation enacted by the United Progressive Alliance (UPA) government led by the Congress party followed a number of civil society campaigns, the filing of public interest litigations in the Supreme Court and a new phase of judicial activism. In direct contrast to the early years of post-Independence India when the court had privileged fundamental rights over the directive principles, the Supreme Court became an ardent advocate of social rights. It began to concentrate on pro-people issues.

The dissenting opinion of Justice P.N. Bhagwati of the Supreme Court in the case of *Minerva Mills vs the Union of India* in 1980 can be seen as important in this context. The issue at hand was whether parliament had unlimited power to amend the Constitution, a power that had been granted by the 42nd Amendment Act passed during Indira Gandhi's Emergency regime in 1976. Specifically, clause 4 of the Act gave the parliament unhindered power to pass legislation securing the directive principles, even if the said law was inconsistent with any of the fundamental rights. The five-judge bench of the Supreme Court, in its majority verdict, struck down clause 4 (as well as clause 5, which dealt with 'laws in respect of anti-national activities') of the Act and ruled that the power of parliament to amend the Constitution is limited, and that it does not have the power to give priority to the directive principles over fundamental rights. The guarantees given by Part

III of the Constitution cannot be infringed to achieve the goals of Part IV, it held. The two sections of the Constitution had to be harmoniously balanced. [77] Justice Bhagwati, in a dissenting opinion, gave primacy to the directive principles. He argued that social rights are substantive rights. A rule that imposed an obligation on the state or an entity, he ruled, was still a legal rule because it prescribed a norm of conduct to be followed by an authority, even if the rule was not enforceable in court.[78] His minority judgement is a matter of controversy because he upheld the Emergency regime. But it proved prescient. In the twenty-first century, the Supreme Court proceeded to intervene in basic livelihood matters such as health, education, shelter and environment. Shylashri Shankar writes that in the first three decades after Independence, Supreme Court judges treated the directive principles as subservient to fundamental rights. But in the 1970s the Court talked of harmony between rights, and by the 1980s and 1990s, read several social rights as part of the fundamental right to live with dignity.[79]

In the first decade of the twenty-first century, civil society organizations mobilized to represent the interests of the most deprived and the most marginalized in the country. Their efforts proved successful and the enactment of social rights followed.[80] In 2001, in response to a public interest litigation filed by the People's Union for Civil Liberties, Rajasthan on widespread hunger in the country, the Supreme Court passed a number of strictures on the National Democratic Alliance (NDA) government headed by Atal Bihari Vajpayee. It was of utmost importance, instructed the highest court in the land, that food should be provided to vulnerable sections of the people. In case of famine there may be shortage of food, observed the court. Today, however, there is scarcity amidst plenty. Food distribution among the very poor and the destitute is scarce and non-existent leading to malnourishment, starvation and other related problems.[81]

The admonishment bore results, and the Bharatiya Janata Party-led coalition government initiated a massive programme of employment generation via the 'Sampoorna Grameen Rozgar Yojana', streamlining the public distribution system in food grains and mandating mid-day meals for school children. The culmination of the campaign was the National Food Security Act, 2013 under the aegis of the UPA.

The campaign for the right to food realized fairly early on that assured employment is an essential precondition for food security simply because it liberates people from dependence on outside agencies. The demand for this right (distinct from the demand for food-for-work programmes) did not raise a new entitlement onto policy agendas. Several employment generation schemes were in existence in some form or the other. But when in December 2005 the long awaited National Rural Employment Guarantee Act (NREGA; now MGNREGA—the Mahatma Gandhi National Rural Employment Guarantee Act) was adopted by parliament, new hope was infused into rural areas that had been stagnating in recent decades. Considered the largest public works employment project in the world, MGNREGA targeted the rural poor effectively, though we find striking heterogeneity in food delivery across states.

Where the right to education is concerned, writes Shankar, a right came before the law. In a famous judgement on the right to education (the case of *Unni Krishnan vs State of Andhra Pradesh* in 1993) the judges even said that in order for a right to be treated as a fundamental right it was not necessary for it to be in the fundamental rights section of the Constitution. Forty-five years after Independence, the court transformed education into a fundamental right for children aged 6–14.[82] In 2002, the Right to Primary Education was made part of Article 21 of the fundamental rights chapter, that is, the right to life, vide the 86th Constitutional Amendment. This was under the NDA government headed by Vajpayee. In 2005, a significant right that was mandated by the UPA government was the right to information.

India certainly did not undergo a social revolution, but in the ten years of UPA rule (2004–14), attention began to be paid to zones of poverty and illbeing through civil society interventions and court rulings. The role of civil society organizations in promoting social legislation in the period cannot be underestimated. What trade unions and political parties, whose hearts ostensibly bleed for the poor could not do since Independence, civil society accomplished in the space of ten years. India was fortunate that the UPA government viewed civil society mobilization favourably. It gave civil society groups in the country enough space to collectively lobby on various issues. The president of the Congress party, Ms Sonia Gandhi, in fact, set up a National Advisory Committee composed of civil society activists and experienced bureaucrats to draft social legislation.[83]

The role of the judiciary is significant because some campaigns for the delivery of social goods, for example, the right to food and the right to primary education have originated from a Supreme Court decision. The Indian state has at times proved more responsive to Court injunctions than to popular representations, compelling more and more groups to invoke judicial activism. On some occasions the court has acted on its own, notably in the case of the right to education. In the case of the right to food, and later employment, the court cracked the whip on the government when a group of activists filed a petition in the court. We have to note, however, that when it came to development projects, attempts by civil society activists have not always been successful. For example, the demand to stay the building of the Narmada dam in Western India, because it had displaced millions of forest dwellers, was defeated in the Court by the splendid majority of one.

Much concern has been expressed about judicial activism because the judiciary is non-representative, and because it tends to tread on the toes of the executive and of elected members of parliament. Some scholars even dismiss such activism as populism, and a mere attempt to refurbish the image of the court after the Emergency, as Upendra Baxi does. Moreover, as Madhav Khosla points out, the Court pushes a model of conditional social rights insofar as it instructs the state to remedy a particular grievance or remedy a particular lack. 'The existence of a violation is conditional upon state action,' he writes. 'Unlike the South African Supreme Court, the Indian Court has not elaborated a doctrine of systemic social rights in the form of an entitlement for everyone.'[84] The failure to do so has enabled the advent of a highly personalized form of delivery of social goods under the rule of the BJP. The economist Arvind

Subramanian has termed this the 'new welfarism', which can be reconceptualized not as welfarism (which presupposes the possession of social rights), but delivery of social goods *from above*.

## The Model of Personalized Welfarism

The political scene changed dramatically in 2014. In the run up to the elections, the Congress rightfully claimed credit for social legislation—the right to food, MGNREGA and the right to information. Yet the party managed to secure only forty-four seats in the popular house of parliament. The winner was the Bharatiya Janata Party that managed on a vote share of 31 per cent to secure 282 seats in the lower house. In the 2019 general elections, the BJP bettered its vote share, which went up to 37 per cent, giving it more than 303 seats in the Lok Sabha.

Though the BJP government has implemented a number of social policy initiatives, the approach of the government to these issues causes concern. The rights-based approach to wellbeing, which had been emphasized by civil society activists during the period the UPA I and II governments were in power (2004–09 and 2009–14, respectively), has been replaced by the enactment of social policy 'from above' in line with East Asian countries, such as Singapore.

Importantly, announcements under this new social welfarism policy have also been accompanied by declining allocations on expenditure and neglect of existing schemes and programmes. For example, in the 2023–24 Union Budget, the Finance Minister cut down allocations for NREGA from 1.11 lakh crores in the 2021 to 60,000 crores.[85] The reduction has been effected despite the fact that during the pandemic lockdown from March to May 2020, it was NREGA that provided livelihood to lakhs of migrant workers who had walked to their villages in search of food.

A recent article in *The Wire*, by Asmi Sharma of Jan Sarokar and Nancy Pathak of the Centre for Financial Accountability, notes that in the last decade we saw not only the rise of crony capitalism, but also 'a discernible dismantling of the welfare and social security framework that provides social and economic protection to crores of citizens'. The Pradhan Mantri Garib Kalyan Anna Yojna was discontinued in January 2023. This resulted in a 50 per cent reduction in ration entitlements for 81 crore people. 'Election gimmicks,' remark the authors, 'such as the cutting down of the price of LPG cylinders, overshadow the lack of substantive and transformative interventions that can genuinely improve welfare.'[86] The noted economist Jean Dreze is of the opinion that the main objective of new policies, which often are little but the renaming of existing policies, appears to be to promote the image of the Prime Minister.[87] And public policy expert Yamini Aiyar writes that what is termed as the new welfarism prioritizes the subsidized public provisioning of *private* over *public* goods. So, instead of the provision of health and education, there is emphasis on direct cash transfers, subsidies for housing, health insurance, toilets and drinking water. This 'preference for private goods has to be understood through the prism of the emergent mode of political branding and the very unique role played by welfare schemes in shaping this [and enabling] a direct connection between the party leadership (the prime minister himself) and the voter. This connection is nurtured through the deification of the leadership by projecting the leader as the sole patron and provider thus enabling the leadership to consolidate power without having to bargain with local leaders and factions.'[88] This, she suggests, is welfare based on loyalty, benevolence, and the persona of the party leadership. She describes it as 'patrimonial welfarism'.

Aiyar makes a valid point. The citizen is recast as the 'labharthi' (beneficiary) rather than a rights-bearing claimant of welfare. Social rights and civil society mobilization that demands social rights have been replaced by the idea of a *consumer* of a handful of grain, entitled to social goods as a personal gift from the Prime Minister. This is completely contrary to the approach that governed welfare legislation in the post-Second World War period in Europe, particularly in Scandinavia, which emphasized the significance of a rights-based approach. This ruled out paternalism and emphasized the rights of citizens to the preconditions of wellbeing. In the first decade of the twenty-first century, it was generally recognized that India had charted out a new route to welfare, that of civil society intervention. From 2001 to 2014, civil society organizations came together in a series of coalitions to press upon the government the need to recognize social rights as legally enforceable rights. These organizations kept watch on the performance of the government. A number of social audit groups issued report cards on how government policy had fared and whether it had been implemented at all.

In the decade that followed we saw the muzzling of civil society. The government came down heavily on non-governmental organizations, blocking their funding, casting doubts on their legitimacy and questioning their very role in democracy. We saw a major truncation of the domestic space of debate and dissent, as the BJP and its front organizations proceeded to monopolize the space of civil society. In effect, the current moment in the biography of social rights is witnessing a sharp reduction of the role of civil society both in the making of policy and in articulating dissent on policies that subvert the foundations of democracy. The turn has serious implications. If India had any claims to moving towards a welfare state model based on the right of the citizen to public goods as the precondition of a good life, these claims have been overset.[89] Also in danger is the right to civil liberties such as freedom of expression and the right to form associations. Delhi was used to the spectacle of people marching in tandem to demand social rights. Today, there are no such processions, and politicians in power in the various states prefer to hand out doles, free bus passes, some money to women, and gas subsidies instead of institutionalizing the realization of the right to social goods.

This is the problem that flows from the dismissal of the notion of redistribution of resources and its replacement by the notion of benevolence by the ruling class. Though we have acknowledged the role of civil society campaigns for social rights that sparked off legislation and propelled judicial activism on this front during the two terms of the UPA government, these campaigns failed to effect a social transformation of the state. This is not surprising. For civil society works within the frame of the system. Civil society organizations might try to push the frontiers of the system, but in general they do not propel mobilization for redistribution of wealth or even conceptualize redistributive justice.

Given the extent of poverty in the country, it is not surprising that even the handing over of a handful of grain to people, who should have been granted the preconditions of—what one of the clauses of Article 21 of our Constitution termed—a life of dignity, is accepted as benevolence. It is not surprising that the imprint of the leadership on this bag of grain convinces people that social goods such as food are made available to them by the generosity of the ruling class. The establishment of a direct relationship between the leader and the people over the heads of institutions that realize social rights is a classic sign of authoritarian populism. The problem is that this relationship reduces the citizen as the bearer of rights to a consumer, who pays for this handful of grain with her vote. This undercuts not only the importance of living a life of dignity that has been promised by the Constitution, it subverts the prime value of equality that the Preamble promises us. In the third decade of the twenty-first century, India might well have regressed from democracy to paternalism and personalized welfare, which characterized feudalism. After all, even feudal nobilities gave to their people a bowl of soup in times of hardship. What they did not give them was rights based on equality and freedom from want, or their right to fight for these goods.

## Chapter V

# We, the People

We, the people, owe each other obligations of justice. This, as suggested earlier, can only be realized when the dry bones of the law are clothed with an emotion we call sympathy or solidarity. This is necessary because someone has to speak back to power when the Constitution is violated. It is undeniable that governments have done so in the past. They have ignored the intellectual labour, the wisdom, the spirit of dialogue and compromise, and above all, the creativity that marked interactions between the members of the Constituent Assembly. It is a credit to these fine minds that their vision of how India should be politically organized, has, to a great extent, endured since Independence in the political imagination of social movements.

### The Constitution—the End of the Politics of Protest?

The Constituent Assembly which was set up in December 1946 was indirectly elected by the provincial assemblies elected earlier in the year. While introducing the Objectives Resolution, Pandit Nehru said:[90] '[T]his Constituent Assembly is not what many of us wished it to be. It has come into being under particular conditions and the British Government ha[d] a hand in its birth. They have attached to it certain conditions. We accepted the State Paper, which may be called the foundation of this Assembly, after serious deliberations and we shall endeavour to work within its limits. But you must not ignore the source from which this Assembly derives its strength... We have met here today because of the strength of the people behind us and we shall go as far as the people...shall wish us to go. We should, therefore, always keep in mind the passions that lie in the hearts of the masses of the Indian people and try to fulfil them.'[91]

'The Resolution', continued Pandit Nehru, 'that I am placing before you is in the nature of a pledge. The Resolution deals with fundamentals which are commonly held and have been accepted by the people. [I]t is our firm and solemn resolve to have a sovereign Indian republic... The Resolution does not go into [the] details. It contains only the fundamentals... Laws are made of words but this Resolution is something higher than the law.'[92] The old order is fast changing, he said, yielding place to the new. We need to look at the spirit behind the word.

The Indian Constitution institutionalized the precepts and the objectives of democracy, the 'fundamentals which are commonly held and have been accepted by the people'. However, as noted earlier in this essay, in the hands of an elite hungry for power, constitutions can be stripped of their prescriptive and regulatory roles. Dr Ambedkar had warned us against precisely this development in his final address on the

Draft Constitution on 25 November 1949. '[H]owever good a Constitution may be,' he remarked, 'it is sure to turn out bad because those who are called to work it, happen to be a bad lot. However bad a Constitution may be, it may turn out to be good if those who are called to work it, happen to be a good lot. The working of a Constitution does not depend wholly upon the nature of the Constitution.' It depends also on the people and on the political parties they elect. 'It is, therefore, futile to pass any judgement upon the Constitution without reference to the part which the people and their parties are likely to play.'[93]

Given the context of the Partition, a divided country needed a new set of norms that went beyond politicized religion in order to be constituted as a political community based on solidarity. A set of norms, which the chairman of the Drafting Committee hoped would, to a greater or lesser extent, prevent our Constitution from 'turn[ing] out bad'. In response to criticism of the Draft Constitution, on 4 November 1948, Ambedkar acknowledged that detailed administrative provisions should ideally not form a part of a constitution. But the inclusion of procedures and processes in the founding document, he insisted, was necessary to protect democracy. For, as he was to say famously, democracy 'in India is only a top-dressing on an Indian soil, which is essentially undemocratic.'[94]

Dr Ambedkar brought great learning, immense political understanding, and insightful perception to the deliberations of the Constituent Assembly. He also brought to the debate vast wisdom born out of his own experiences as a Dalit. Life had taught him that it was not enough for the people to give themselves a constitution. The constitution needed to become a part of their lives. It needed to be an object of reverence and of political passion. This virtue he called constitutional morality.

Ambedkar's inspiration for the concept of constitutional morality was the nineteenth century British historian and Enlightenment thinker, George Grote (1794–1871). Grote had authored twelve volumes on the history of Greece (published between 1846 and 1856), particularly on Athenian democracy. Intent on defending Athenian democracy against its critics like Plato and others, Grote suggested that Athens had given to the world a notion of democracy that rested on the twin planks of freedom and self-restraint. He focused on Cleisthenes, whom he considered to be the founder of Athenian democracy, and on his belief that we must be passionately attached to the constitution. The idea was to replace arbitrary decision-making by the institutionalization of procedures.

The coexistence of freedom and self-imposed restraints, for Grote, can be found in two other historical instances. The first was the Glorious Revolution in England in 1688–89. This bloodless 'revolution' marked the triumph of Parliament, which replaced the monarch James II with his daughter Mary II and her husband William III on the throne. This was confirmed by the adoption of the Bill of Rights, 1969. The Bill truncated the power of the monarch.

The second such instance for Grote was the enactment of the American constitution, when the USA declared itself free of England. It was an instance of the victory of democracy marked by the rule of law, and the morality of the constitution.

There was a deeper argument that underlay the idea of constitutional morality best expressed in the words of Grote. 'It was necessary [for Cleisthenes] to create in the multitude...that rare and difficult sentiment which we may term constitutional morality—a paramount reverence for the forms of the constitution, enforcing obedience to the authorities, acting under and within these forms, yet combined with the habit of open speech, of action subject only to definite legal control and unrestrained censure of those very authorities as to all their public acts—combined too with a perfect confidence in the bosom of every citizen amidst the bitterness of a party contest, that the form of the constitution will not be less sacred in the eyes of the opponents than his own.'[95]

Political authorities, in other words, were responsible for the inculcation of this political virtue; a virtue that the Victorians called 'character'. Grote's critics allege that his 'apologia' for Athens was not about Athenians but about his own generation. It was about Victorians who respected character polished by thrift, industry and prudishness. The eminent historian E.H. Carr, in his famous lectures on *What is History?*, wrote that Grote, an enlightened radical banker writing in the 1840s, embodied the aspirations of the rising and politically progressive British middle class in an idealized picture of Athenian democracy. In his story of Athens, Pericles figured as a Benthamite reformer, and the democratic city-state of Athens acquired an empire in a fit of absence of mind. 'It may not be fanciful to suggest that Grote's neglect of the problem of slavery in Athens reflected the failure of the group to which he belonged to face the problem of the new English factory working class.'[96]

Dr Ambedkar did not replicate Grote's omission of slavery, or indeed of women and aliens from his depiction of democracy.

He was far too conscious of the many oppressions and the many tyrannies of a caste-bound society. The only way out of a hierarchical society was constitutional morality which could override socially discriminatory laws, taboos and regulations and at the same time promote a sense of freedom. This, he hoped, would ensure restraint on the exercise of power. In sum, only when society was saturated with constitutional morality could we take the risk of omitting the details of administration in the Constitution, Ambedkar argued.

But can we presume, asked Ambedkar in a rhetorical master-stroke, that there is diffusion of constitutional morality in India? For constitutional morality has to be cultivated; it is not a natural sentiment. The power elite had to, as Grote had theorized, '*create* in the multitude...that rare and difficult sentiment which we may term constitutional morality—a paramount reverence for the forms of the constitution'. Since Indian society was profoundly undemocratic, a government that was passionately attached to the morality of the constitution had to take up the task of inculcating and fostering this sentiment.

This was prudent from the perspective of the ruling class, because constitutional morality bred moderate politics. Otherwise societies will land up, as Grote had warned, with the sort of excesses that were bred by the French Revolution. 'The many violences', Grote had written, 'of the first French revolution illustrates among other lessons, the fatal effects arising from its absence, even among a people high in the scale of intelligence.'[97]

Dr Ambedkar shared this suspicion of unguarded and radical political action. Clashes of interest had to be resolved within the framework of the Constitution. Since the adoption of the Constitution heralded the transition from subject to citizen, the transition, for him, marked the end of agitational politics. Since the 1920s, mass movements had succeeded in challenging the colonial government on practically every policy. Now it was time for Indians to move from the politics of protest to the politics of responsible citizenship within the framework of the Constitution.

The transition would be undoubtedly difficult. People belonging to diverse persuasions had mobilized under the flag of non-cooperation, civil disobedience, the Salt Satyagraha and Quit India. Could they begin to work with each other to realize democratic ideals quite in the same way in an undemocratic society? We could do so suggested Ambedkar, on 25 November 1949, only if we 'hold fast to constitutional methods of achieving our social and economic objectives. It must mean that we abandon the bloody methods of revolution. It means we must abandon the method of civil disobedience, non-cooperation and satyagraha'.[98]

Arguably, the end of the politics of protest, whether revolutionary or peaceful, can also imply the end of history. History hardly gives us an instance of a perfect post-political order, except for relatively short periods under tyrants. Politics is an inherent feature of all human collectivities, ranging from the household to the state to the global order. Whether political/collective action affirms power, moderates it, or rejects it in favour of a more humane society, what must be recognized is that human beings are political by nature. This is more than evident in India's history.

### Civil Society and the Restoration of the Constitution

Once independence had been attained, society quietened down for about twenty years. Indians trusted leaders who headed the state; these were the same leaders who had inspired and led the freedom struggle. Things changed by the late 1960s. A generation born after Independence had come to maturity, and this generation demanded wellbeing from the government, which had failed to deliver. In 1974–75, the socialist leader Jaya Prakash Narayan tapped simmering discontent and mobilized the youth to protest against the misgovernance of Indira Gandhi's government. Starting in Bihar, the movement soon spread out to the rest of the country. The latter suspended civil liberties in June 1975. Thousands of Indians were imprisoned. In the general elections that followed after the Emergency was lifted in January 1977, the government was defeated and a coalition under the name of the Janata Party came to power. The people of India had learnt their lesson. Without a vibrant and vigilant civil society governments can easily misuse power and suppress the rights of the people. The Constitution protected the citizens; it was also the duty of citizens to protect the Constitution.

After the Emergency was lifted, India saw an eruption of civil society organizations. Whereas the last years of the 1960s witnessed the surge of a violent Naxalite movement in Bengal and later in other parts of the country, civil society organizations worked within the parameters of the Constitution. The demand of civil society was simply this: give us what has been promised by the Constitution. Civil society had recognized the great importance of the right to life and liberty, the right to freedom of expression and the right to protest. As remarked earlier, a hungry human being cannot be free, but a citizen who is not hungry is also not free if her civil liberties are taken away. Organizations for the protection of women's rights, for Dalit rights, and movements against communalism raised significant issues onto the public domain.

If the Constitution grants the right to life to all citizens vide Article 21, the state has to grant to all citizens certain preconditions for living a good life. Within a short period of time the range of these preconditions had expanded from health, education and employment, to the right to environment, and the right not to be displaced from one's habitat. Big development projects, by damaging the environment—introducing deadly chemicals into the soil, depleting forests, polluting rivers and poisoning the atmosphere—thus were seen to pose a threat to people's basic rights. Civil society organizations had been working among marginalized populations for sometime, for example, forest dwellers and others, who were not necessarily forest dwellers, but who lived off natural resources while also conserving the environment, causing far less damage than modern technology would.

One movement, which began in the mid-1980s and soon caught the imagination of the people, was one that brought to the centre-stage these very issues—the environment, the rights of tribal communities not to be displaced and the hazards of big development projects. It was sparked off by the building of the Narmada dam that affected people in Gujarat, Maharashtra and Madhya Pradesh, displacing thousands of Adivasis from their habitat, harnessing the mighty Narmada river but inundating forest land and destroying the delicate environmental balance. It did not enhance the quality of life for the tribal community that was alienated from its land, modes of agriculture and natural resources. The political plank of the Narmada Bachao Andolan addressed not only these issues, it put onto the table the issue of preconditions to a good life. It asked why the interests of the tribals had been ignored when big development projects were being planned.

The NBA generated a wide-ranging and exhilarating debate on the notion of development across the country. Engineers, architects, development experts, activists, academics and journalists discussed, debated and disagreed on the advantages and the disadvantages of large dams weighed against the rights of forest dwellers. The scale of mobilization was inspiring; the scale of debate over the ambiguous notion of development even more so. Research scholars completed doctorates on these issues, books were written on the theme, and the movement even attracted attention internationally. The no-dam stance of its leaders dovetailed into an incisive critique of development by the global community of non-governmental organizations.

The movement perfected the art of non-violent struggle. Medha Patkar stood in the swirling waters of the Narmada river for days to protest against raising the height of the dam, because that would displace even more Adivasis. Participants went on hunger strikes, demonstrated in front of the World Bank that had given a loan to the Indian government to build the dam, and as the farmers' movement would do many years later, stoically bore the most virulent of criticism. The Narmada

Bachao Andolan lost its case before the Supreme Court, but the activists continue to fight for the right of forest communities not to be displaced and offer alternative notions of development to enhance people's quality of life. They wanted the benefits the Constitution had granted to its citizens to be extended to those communities that were marginalized. Among the marginalized were those affected by big development projects.

### *The Anti-CAA Protests*

One of the most dramatic manifestations of the right to protest for the interests of our fellow citizens in India's recent history was witnessed in 2019. Facilitated by a 'brute majority' in the Lok Sabha, the BJP government proceeded to legislate policies that are at best questionable. On 9 December 2019, the government introduced the Citizenship Amendment Bill (CAB) in the lower house of parliament. The Bill introduced the dangerous and discriminatory idea of making the grant of Indian citizenship dependent on the religion an individual belonged to. Cleared by the cabinet in December 2018, the Citizenship Amendment Act, which was passed by parliament on 11 December 2019, grants the right to Indian citizenship to non-Muslim refugees who seek to escape religious persecution in Pakistan, Bangladesh and Afghanistan, countries where Islam is the official religion.

The Act aroused a storm of protest. Commentators argued that the connection that the government established between citizenship and religion violates the Constitution of India. India wanted to provide a home to refugees fleeing religious persecution in neighbouring countries, but the Ahmadiyyas, who are non-citizens in Pakistan, and Hazaras who face religious discrimination in Afghanistan, it was pointed out, had not been given this option.

The linking of religion and citizenship held serious implications for the rights of the Muslim minority because the proposed National Population Register and a National Register of Citizens intended to weed out what were called 'infiltrators' or refugees. The Muslim community was racked by uncertainty and anxiety since its members could potentially be declared non-citizens, or worse, illegal migrants, if unable produce the required documents, which a huge population of Indians simply do not have.

The opposition in parliament had dwindled to nothing and civil society organizations had been hammered into inaction. The political implications were ominous. Who could confront the holders of power who had set themselves up as arbiters of citizenship?

And then the political miracle happened. On 15 December 2019, students belonging to the Jamia Millia Islamia in Delhi came out in large numbers to protest against the Citizenship Amendment Act. Their procession carried banners that rejected the CAA, and demanded its withdrawal. They were subjected to police violence and the university was ransacked. The incident sparked off massive protests led by university students across the country.

The rest of India watched with amazement and great admiration this unexpected political spectacle of performative citizenship. Indians, young and not so young, marched holding the national flag in one hand, and copies of the Constitution in the other. They marched peacefully and assembled peacefully in public spaces. They sang the national anthem, and recited revolutionary poetry, particularly Faiz Ahmad Faiz's poem titled 'Hum Dekhenge' (We will see!). Pictures of Bhagat Singh, Gandhi and Ambedkar provided the background for their protest.

As political performance, these protests could be remarkably creative and imaginative. Students, for example, went around offering roses to flummoxed police personnel. Photographs in the morning newspapers and videos screened by television channels bore witness to the democratic nature of the protest—a young woman holding up a gentle admonishing finger to the police, novel art forms that concentrated on the plurality of India and the determination of citizens to protect it, the national flag painted on the cheeks of little children, chants of solidarity with Muslim fellow citizens. Young people read out the Preamble of the Constitution that promises liberty, equality and justice. Through such public enactment of the Preamble, they transformed the Constitution into a public, accessible and democratic document. The Constitution, they reiterated, is the anchor of our identity, the protector of our rights, our legacy and our culture. The occupation of public spaces, sit-downs on public roads and the coinage of innovative slogans realized, proclaimed and enacted popular sovereignty.

William Wordsworth had written on the French Revolution thus: 'Bliss was it in that dawn to be alive / But to be young was very heaven.' Given the looming clouds of fear that the government would use violence, the enthusiasm of the young reminded us of these very lines. The sit-in by women, some of them elderly grandmothers, in Shaheen Bagh in South Delhi for over ninety days, became a symbol of protest across the world.

No political party had launched a protest march against the CAA worth its name, no politician had gone on a fast in opposition to the law, and a compliant media had played down the discriminatory nature of the legislation. In such adverse circumstances, our young citizens reinvented a notion that had gone missing—that of sympathy and solidarity with fellow citizens.

Never has India seen the enactment of citizenship on this scale. These protests were not against the grant of citizenship to outsiders. They were a recognition that the provisions of the Act would set the ground for further disenfranchisement of Muslim citizens. In the process, young Indians reiterated the right to protest, to assemble peacefully and without arms, and the right to share equally in the burdens and the benefits that a society has to offer. They reasserted the right of citizens to hold an elected government accountable for discriminatory laws.

The key issue brought forth was: can citizenship be reduced to what European activists call 'papier citizenship', or paper citizenship, which depends on us having *necessary* documents?

The Constitution authorizes us to benefit from the security and the services provided by the state—education, health, housing, post-retirement benefits, the right to travel, the right to employment and, above all, the right to vote. But there is more to citizenship. Citizenship is a relational concept because it establishes a bond between us. The bond is not based on blood but on belonging to a civic community defined by the Constitution. Protesting against their potential disenfranchisement, these young people were out not only to protect their fellow citizens, they were there to protect the Indian Constitution.

For five and a half years the ruling party had appropriated the symbols of nationhood, collapsed the democratic state into the nation, the nation into the government, and the government into the leader. Any protest against the government or the leader was thus typed as anti-national. The anti-CAA protests enacted the basic rule of citizenship that rulers often forget, that 'We, the People of India' are the real repositories of power. The government is elected by us and is responsible to us. The right to citizenship was re-appropriated in 2019, popular sovereignty reclaimed, the Constitution held up as our protection and our guide to political practices, and the government was put in its place. Citizens told the government that they will not tolerate any tampering with the Constitution. They proclaimed that the right to citizenship is theirs by reason of birth, by reason of belonging, by reason of fidelity, by reason of solidarity with fellow citizens, and for the simple reason that they bow their heads before the national flag and stand up in reverence when the national anthem is sung.

The onslaught of communal riots in North-East Delhi in the last half of February 2020 put a sudden end to popular protest. In March 2020, the pandemic swept the country pushing people back into their homes and stripping public spaces of any vestige of protest. The massive movement launched by our students was halted. But it left a rich legacy. No matter how authoritarian a government might be, people can always resort to protest against laws that are discriminatory, in order to preserve our Constitution.

### *The Farmers' Struggle*

Another significant movement in recent history was launched by farmers in 2020. This was an important watershed in the history of social movements. Thousands of farmers assembled on the outskirts of Delhi. They wanted the farm laws passed in September 2020 to be withdrawn. These laws sought to reshape farming in India by minimizing the role of the government in agriculture, and opening the sphere of agriculture to private investment. The government justified the laws on the ground that private investment would increase agricultural growth. The farmers rightly feared that the new market-friendly laws would remove the protection of the state from agriculture and leave the farmers at the mercy of large corporations. Alongside, the demonstrators asked the government to protect their livelihoods through other means such as a minimum support price. This was again a demand for the fulfilment of the right to a life worth living.

The visual and the political impact of the assembly was extraordinary. So was the scale of the movement led initially by farmers from Punjab, Haryana and Uttar Pradesh. Within a short period of time farmers from other states joined in to create a spectacular struggle for basic wellbeing and state protection. We witnessed once again the recovery of agency in times of authoritarianism. The movement demonstrated that ordinary people possess the political competence to evaluate laws, to judge an elected government, participate in the decision-making process and, if this is denied to them, to exercise their right to protest.

The moment protestors occupy public land, space is transformed into a site of struggle. This struggle imprints onto space the fundamental understanding that politics is contestation. What is not contested is not politics. Social movements demand a different sort of politics, a more caring politics based on sympathy and solidarity, one that is sensitive to the needs and the travails of vulnerable sections of society. By joining such a struggle, protestors come to acquire agency, thus reinforcing their status as bearers of rights, especially the right to freedom of expression and the right to assemble peacefully. The act of entering the public sphere is in itself a declaration: *This is who I am. This is what I stand for.* The process of justifying their stand makes individuals a part of a community, related to others by virtue of espousing the same cause. From a random collection of individual citizens, the people become a collective determined to realize the promises of their Constitution.

The farmers' struggle forged solidarity among different sections of the farming class, and also between the farmers and other Indians. We noted with surprise and delight the development of a massive support system that clustered around the movement. Many demonstrators in the movement were not agriculturalists. Yet they were ready to defy the power of the Indian government. Numerous groups set up *langars* or meals, provided tents, health facilities and small shopping areas for everyday needs. They played and sang the music of protest. Farmers planted flowers on their side of barbed wire barricades erected by the police; some among them took up the responsibility of recording day-to-day activities, drafting petitions and demands, and talking to journalists; others strategized and yet others conferred with government representatives.

All of them bore stoically the infamies that were heaped on their heads by the cheer leaders of the ruling party. Protestors braved epithets, slogans that denigrated them and allegations that they were nothing but instruments of separatism and terrorism. They collectively mourned the death of their own. In one case, that of their comrades brutally run over and killed by an SUV allegedly driven by functionaries of the ruling party in Lakhimpur Kheri in Uttar Pradesh. They withstood the blazing heat of Delhi summers, the crippling cold of winters, and torrential rains that reduced the site of struggle to slush. But they persisted.

Like other struggles, the farmers' struggle inspired an informed debate on the rights of agriculturalists to be protected by the state. The scale and the intensity of political protest stirred imaginations and energized other people here and abroad. And the struggle was victorious. The Prime Minister finally agreed to withdraw the three laws that corporatized agriculture in November 2021.

~

The link which connects individuals into a collective may be purely transitional and purely ephemeral. It does not matter. What is important is that, through protest, these movements create a 'we, the people'. They wrest the phrase from the cloying palms of power elites who use the term 'people' to justify injustice. They do so by claiming that they speak and act in the name of the people. Social movements have shown us that popular sovereignty granted by the Constitution, i.e. 'we, the people', is reclaimed in and through protest and solidarity. This sends a signal to the world. It is possible for ordinary individuals to make history through the transformation of public spaces into political spaces and through reclaiming popular sovereignty and re-locating it in the people. These messages are not inconsequential. They bear great implications for democratic theory and practice. If we value constitutional democracy we must be prepared to struggle.

# An Afterword

## *The Way Things Are and the Way They Should Be*

Dr Ambedkar had hoped that we would, after Independence, make use of 'constitutional methods of achieving our social and economic objectives'. But he also acknowledged that, in the wrong hands, the Constitution would be distorted. When that did happen in India's post-colonial history, the people had to once again resort to methods of civil disobedience. And it was the Constitution which formed the axis around which the political community revolved.

The invocation of constitutional provisions by social activists is important, because we have to admit that the record of constitutionalism in India is mixed. This is perhaps not surprising. Political power is heady. The holders of power are often more interested in the implementation of their party agendas than in upholding the constitutional mandate; they disdain limits on their authority. They sweep aside public opinion, ride roughshod over social movements, repress civil society activism, jail dissenters, violate civil liberties at will and in general behave as if power is their passport to eternity.

The basic principles of democracy—the separation of power and checks and balances—have been infringed with some impunity in India. The internal Emergency of 1975–77, and the violation of the fundamental rights of the people of the Northeast and of Jammu and Kashmir by the imposition of the Armed Forces (Special Powers) Act, within a few years of the promulgation of the Constitution, form some of the most egregious examples. But regulatory agencies have been routinely brought under the sway of the executive, parliament has often been reduced to a talking shop, civil society has been pulverized, and the Constitution has been amended over a hundred times. What, then, is the value of the Constitution?

Arguably, the Constitution holds more value for citizens than for governments. It enables us to comprehend the distinction between the way 'things are' and the way 'things should be'. Governments might dishonour the Constitution, but at the same time, social movements draw inspiration from the founding document of the republic when they resist the exercise of arbitrary power, when they seek to realize its promise that, ultimately, power rests with the people.

A word in caution might be necessary here. Though the phrase 'we, the people' is a powerful indicator of popular sovereignty, it is not self-explanatory. The distinguished jurist Sir Ivor Jennings had famously announced that the principle of self-determination that declares, 'Let the people decide,' was ridiculous. 'The people,' he remarked, 'cannot decide until somebody decides who are the people.' The people is not a demographic category which includes each and every individual who lives within the territorial boundaries of a country. It is a political concept which embodies popular sovereignty.

We need to reassert the constitutional provision of popular sovereignty because if the politics of power can be inclusive, it can also be exclusionary. Governments can easily render large sections of 'the people' politically irrelevant, by labelling them illegal immigrants, or aliens, or immigrants, or the enemy, or even as termites, thus denying them their political rights. And then they can turn around and tell *us* that they speak, legislate and govern in the name of *the people*. We might have to conclude, on a pessimistic note, that ultimately the question of who the people are is decided by cynical calculations of power, since it has been conveniently appropriated by governments seeking to legitimize power in the name of the same people they oppress.

Edmund Morgan, in his *Inventing the People: The Rise of Popular Sovereignty in England and America*, labels the notion of the people as a political fiction that was invented to challenge and replace another fiction—the divine right of kings. During the English Civil War 'representatives invented the sovereignty of the people in order to claim it for themselves... In the name of the people they became all-powerful in government'.[99] The interpretation is persuasive, particularly when we recollect how often the phrase is invoked to validate disturbing and contentious policies.

Elite appropriations of a phrase that lies at the heart of democracy—and which forms the opening sentence of our Constitution—is not all that surprising. Whereas the exercise of governmental power reinforces relations of domination and subordination, power hungry politicians want more. They want to secure their own future by producing compliant *subjects* out of citizens, and by shaping the social order to fit their ambitions and party ideologies. The people elect the government; it is they that should be holding the governments they have elected to account. When a collective called the people speaks, elected leaders should be listening. Astute power holders hollow out the phrase and reduce it to a legitimizing strategy when they *create* 'the people' by appropriating democratic languages and practices. And sadly, 'we, the people' often do not even recognize how we have been manipulated by ignoble ideologies and by cynical politicians who play upon social insecurities and vulnerabilities in our name.

Fortunately, history tells us that no story of power can be abstracted from resistance. Someone, somewhere will stand up and protest against laws that threaten livelihoods and lives. Somebody will read the words of the Preamble of the Constitution in public, and spark off a major social movement that re-appropriates notions of popular sovereignty. He or she will legitimize the protest in the name of the Constitution, help re-appropriate democratic vocabularies and wrest them out of the closed fists of politicians.

At the risk of repetition: politics is always contested; what is not contested cannot be political. Sometimes contestation over political meanings can take the form of everyday resistance, like landless labour refusing to work in the fields, or strikes, fasts and processions. On occasion, contestation is expressed through larger social movements that bring people together to protest and author an alternative politics. Embodied within the imaginaries and the languages of the movement is a more democratic and a more humane notion of politics. We are of course speaking of a movement that is inclusive in its breadth and breathtaking in its vision of freedom, like the ones we discussed in chapter five.

The onset of such a protest movement inaugurates a new phase of politics in a different mode. As people come together and occupy public spaces, through sheer togetherness they demonstrate the power of alternative forms of politics. They reinvent the notion of popular sovereignty. The very act of assembling in public spaces to protest and to create reminds us of the philosopher Hannah Arendt's suggestion that politics demands not only spaces where people can assemble, but also the physical appearance of bodies. This is an essential precondition of action.

Civil society does not revolt against state power. All it demands is that power should be exercised according to certain procedures established by the Constitution, that rights should trump every other consideration, that the rule of law ought to override arbitrary decision-making and that the government exists for the people. Elected governments are bound to secure wellbeing by the creation of the preconditions of a good life. When governments go wrong, as they tend to do periodically, every citizen should be able to state firmly: *This is in violation of the Constitution!* Every citizen should be able to demand basic goods such as employment, food, education and health services because that is our democratic right. We do not get food by the charity of leaders who personalize power; the government is obliged to care for the wellbeing of its people. If it does not do so, every citizen should be able to say as the Red Queen of Hearts said in *Alice in Wonderland*: 'Off with their heads!' speaking of course purely metaphorically.

The Constitution is ours, forged through blood and sweat. It was given to us by ourselves. It is part of our collective consciousness as a political community. It is our identity. It is our referral for evaluating the performance of the government, and it is our guide and inspiration. Our leaders should be wary of what Greek mythology called hubris. Hubris refers to the overweening pride and arrogance of people in power. It is precisely hubris that, in this genre of mythology, was overturned by the avenging goddess, Nemesis, the sister of Justitia, the Goddess of Justice. It is no wonder that the Constitution has become the defender of people's rights time and again. It is no wonder that governments which exercise enormous power have been defeated at the hustings.

# Suggested Readings

Austin, Granville, *The Indian Constitution: Cornerstone of a Nation*, Oxford: Clarendon Press, 1966

Baxi, Upendra, *The Crisis of the Indian Legal System*, New Delhi: Vikas, 1985

Carr, E.H., *What is History?*, The George Macaulay Trevelyan Lectures delivered in the University of Cambridge, January—March 1961, UK, Penguin Books

Constituent Assembly Debates, Official Reports, New Delhi: Lok Sabha Secretariat, 1989

Gandhi, M.K., 'Speech on Fundamental Rights', 31 March 1931, The Collected Works of Mahatma Gandhi, volume XLV, New Delhi: Ministry of Information and Broadcasting, Publications Division, 1971, pp. 372–74

Jacobsohn, Gary, *The Wheel of Law: India's Secularism in Comparative and Constitutional Context*, New Delhi: Oxford University Press, 2003

Jain, M.P., 'The Supreme Court and Fundamental Rights', in S.K Verma and K. Kusum, ed., *Fifty Years of the Supreme Court of India*, New Delhi: Indian Law Institute and Oxford University Press, 2000

Khosla, Madhav, 'Making social rights conditional: lessons from India', *International Journal of Constitutional Law*, vol. 8, no. 4 (2010), pp. 739–65

Kierstead, James, 'Grote's Athens: The Character of Democracy', in Kyriakos N. Demetriou, ed., *Brill Companion to George Grote*, Leiden: Brill, 2014, pp. 161–210

Kumar, Ravinder, and Hari Deo Sharma, *Selected Works of Motilal Nehru*, volume VI, Delhi: Nehru Memorial Museum and Library and Vikas Publishing House, 1995

Morgan, Edmund, *Inventing the People: The Rise of Popular Sovereignty in England and America*, New York: WW Norton and Company, 1988, pp. 49–50

Nehru, Jawharlal, 'A Common Cultural Inheritance', in *Selected Works of Jawaharlal Nehru*, Second Series, Volume 5, New Delhi: Oxford University Press, 1987, pp. 24–26

___, 'A Secular State', in S Gopal, ed., *Jawaharlal Nehru: An Anthology*, Delhi: Oxford University Press, 1980, pp 330–1

___, 'Notes on Minorities', in S. Gopal, ed., *Nehru: Selected Works*, volume 4, Delhi: Jawaharlal Nehru Memorial Fund and Sangam Books, 1976, pp. 259–60

Pandey, Gyanendra, *The Construction of Communalism in North India*, New Delhi: Oxford University Press, 2006

Pannikar, K.N., ed., *Towards Freedom: Documents on the Movement for Independence in India, 1940*, Part 1, Delhi: Indian Council of Historical Research, Oxford University Press, 2009

Parekh, Bhikhu, 'Some reflections on the Hindu theory of tolerance', *Seminar*, 2003

Sen, Ronojoy, *Articles of Faith, Religion, Secularism and the Indian Supreme Court*, New Delhi: Oxford University Press, 2010

Shankar, Shylashri, *Scaling Justice: India's Supreme Court, Anti-Terror Laws and Social Rights*, New Delhi: Oxford University Press, 2009

Shiva Rao, B., *The Framing of India's Constitution: Select Documents*, Volume I, New Delhi: Indian Institute of Public Administration, 1966

Smith, Adam, *The Theory of Moral Sentiments*, edited and with an introduction by D.D. Raphael and A.L. Macfie (1759 edition), Oxford: Clarendon, 1976

Surendranath, Anup, 'Life and Personal Liberty', in Sujit Chowdhry, Madhav Khosla and Pratap Bhanu Mehta, eds, *The Oxford Handbook of the Indian Constitution*, Delhi: Oxford University Press, 2016, pp. 756–76

Thucydides, 'The Pelopennesian War', in *The History of the Peloponnesian War*, translated by Richard Crawley, revised by R. Feetham, *Great Books of the Western World*, editor-in-chief, Mortimer J. Adler, *Encyclopaedia Britannica*, 1990, pp. 345–616

# Endnotes

1 Julian Go, 'Modeling the State: Postcolonial Constitutions in Asia and Africa', *South East Asian Studies,* vol. 30, no. 4 (March), p. 577.

2 Personal communication to the author on 2 October 2023.

3 *Constituent Assembly Debates* (hereinafter *CAD*), volume I, Delhi: Lok Sabha Secretariat, 1989, p. 57.

4 *CAD*, Volume I, p. 60.

5 *CAD*, Volume VII, pp. 37–38.

6 B. Shiva Rao et al., *The Framing of India's Constitution: A Study*, Volume I, New Delhi: Indian Institute of Public Administration, 1966, pp. 5–14.

7 Ibid., p. 5.

8 'The Commonwealth of India Bill', in ibid. pp 43–50.

9 Ibid., pp 43-44

10 Ibid.

11 The other members were Sir Tej Bahadur Sapru, Sir Ali Imam, Syt Pradhan, Syt Shuaib Qureshi, Syt Subhas Chandra Bose, Syt Madhao Shrihari Aney, Syt M.R. Jayakar, Syt N.M. Joshi, and Sardar Mangal Singh. 'All Parties Conference 1928: Report of the Committee', in *Selected Works of Motilal Nehru*, volume VI, edited by Ravinder Kumar and Hari Deo Sharma, Delhi: Nehru Memorial Museum and Library and Vikas Publishing House, 1995, pp 19–20.

12 Ibid., p. 155.

13 Granville Austin, *The Indian Constitution: Cornerstone of a Nation*, Oxford: Clarendon Press, 1966, p. 55.

14 *Selected Works of Motilal Nehru*, op. cit., volume VI, p. 70.

15 Ibid., pp. 155–57.

16 Ibid., pp. 219–20.

17 'Congress Resolution on the White Paper and the Communal Award', in Shiva Rao, op. cit., pp 77–78.

18 M.K. Gandhi, 'The Only Way', 1939, *Collected Works of Mahatma Gandhi* (hereinafter *CWMG*), volume LXXVII, pp. 362–63.

19 Ibid., p. 363.

20 See 'Government of India Act 1935', on Constitution of India (website) (https://www.constitutionofIndia.net/historical-constitution/government-of-india-act-1935/; accessed on 14 November 2023).

21 Shiva Rao, op cit, p 80.

22 Ibid., p. 81.

23 Cited in K.N. Pannikkar (ed.), *Towards Freedom: Documents on the Movement for Independence in India*, Part 1, Delhi: Indian Council of Historical Research and Oxford University Press, pp. 82–83.

24 Shiva Rao, op. cit., p. 250.

25 'Cabinet Mission Plan', in ibid., pp. 208–45, pp. 210–11.

26 Ibid., pp. 208–18, p. 213.

27 Ibid., pp. 213–15.

28 'Congress Resolution Accepting the Cabinet Mission Plan', in ibid., p. 279.

29 *CAD*, Volume I, pp. 60–61.

30 Granville Austin, op. cit., p. 10.

31 *CAD*, Volume XI, p. 974.

32 Granville Austin, op cit, p 12\

33 M.P. Jain, 'The Supreme Court and Fundamental Rights', in *Fifty Years of the Supreme Court of India*, edited by S.K. Verma and K. Kusum, New Delhi: Indian Law Institute and Oxford University Press, 2000, pp. 1–100, p. 22.

34 Ibid., p. 24.

35 Jain, op. cit., p. 31.

36 Anup Surendranath, 'Life and Personal Liberty', in *The Oxford Handbook of the Indian Constitution*, edited by Sujit Chowdhry, Madhav Khosla and Pratap Bhanu Mehta, Delhi: Oxford University Press, 2016, p. 756.

37 *CAD*, volume XI, p. 979.

38 Ibid.

39 Anthony Jay, *The Oxford Dictionary of Political Quotations*, Oxford: Oxford University Press, 2012, p. 323.

40 Dhananjay Mahapatra, 'Significance of SC's minority judgements and their place in polity', *The Times of India*, 15 July 2019.

41 AIR 1976 SC 1207, para 154.

42 AIR 1973 SC 1461.

43 *CAD*, Volume I, p. 50.

44 Adam Smith, *The Theory of Moral Sentiments*, edited and with an introduction by D.D. Raphael and A.L. Macfie (1759 edition), Oxford: Clarendon, 1976, p. 9.

45 Neera Chandhoke, *Rethinking Pluralism, Secularim and Tolerance: Anxieties of Coexistence*, Delhi: Sage, 2015, pp. 111–33.

46 Jawaharlal Nehru, 'Notes on Minorities', in *Nehru: Selected Works*, edited by S. Gopal, volume 4, Delhi: Jawaharlal Nehru Memorial Fund and Sangam Books, 1976, pp 259–60.

47 Gyanendra Pandey, *The Construction of Communalism in North India*, New Delhi: Delhi, Oxford University Press, 2006, p. 250.

48 M.K. Gandhi, 'Speech on Fundamental Rights', 31 March 1931, *CWMG*, volume LI, p. 329.

49 Ibid., p. 330.

50 *CAD*, Volume X, pp. 439, 444, 446.

51 Ibid., p. 441.

52 Ibid., Volume VII, pp. 399–400.

53 Ibid., pp. 401–2. 'It was somewhat new to me,' responded K.T. Shah on the same day, 'to hear that a constitution is a mechanism for regulating the various organs of Government and their functions; and that any desire to include in it any aspiration of the people might be regarded as somewhat out of place.'

54 Ibid., p. 548.

55 It can be argued that the suggestion of Ambedkar for control over religion is the source of the essential practices doctrine that judges have used to evaluate religious practices. Ibid., p. 781.

56 Cited in Robert D. Baird, 'Religion and the Legitimation of Nehru's Concept of the Secular State', in *Religion and the Legitimation of Power in South Asia*, edited by Bardwell L. Smith, Leiden: E.J Brill, 1978, pp. 73–87, p. 80.

57 Jawaharlal Nehru, 'A Common Cultural Inheritance', in *Selected Works of Jawaharlal Nehru*, Second Series, volume 5, New Delhi: Oxford University Press, 1987, p. 26.

58 Jawaharlal Nehru, in *Jawaharlal Nehru: An Anthology*, edited by S. Gopal, Delhi: Oxford University Press, 1980, p. 327.

59 Neera Chandhoke, *Beyond Secularism: The Rights of Religious Minorities*, Delhi: Oxford University Press, 1999, p. 59.

60 Ibid., p. 61.

61 Ibid., p. 56.

62 *Times of India*, 28 October 2016, p. 14.

63 Much of the discussion of the *Bommai* case has been drawn from Gary Jacobsohn, *The Wheel of Law: India's Secularism in Comparative and Constitutional Context*, New Delhi: Oxford University Press, 2003, pp. 145–51.

64 Ibid.

65 Bhikhu Parekh, 'Some reflections on the Hindu theory of tolerance', *India Seminar*, 2003 (available on: https://www.india-seminar.com/2003/521/521%20bhikhu%20parekh.htm; accessed on 19 November 2023).

66 See Ronojoy Sen, *Articles of Faith, Religion, Secularism and the Indian Supreme Court*, New Delhi: Oxford University Press, 2010, p. 22.

67 *CAD*, Volume III, p. 505.

68 Sen, op. cit., p. 221.

69 Dinyar Patel, *Naoroji: Pioneer of Indian Nationalism*, Cambridge: Harvard University Press, 2020.

70 Chris Bayly, *Recovering Liberties: Indian Thought in the Age of Liberalism and Empire*, Cambridge: Cambridge University Press, 2012, p. 1.

71 Rajendra Vora, 'Two Strands of Indian Liberalism: The Ideas of Ranade and Phule', in *Political Thought in Modern India*, edited by Thomas Pantham and Kenneth L. Deutsch, Delhi: Sage, pp. 92–109, pp. 93–96.

72 Cited in Niraja G. Jayal, *Citizenship and Its Discontents*, Cambridge: Harvard University Press, 2013, p. 138.

73 Ravinder Kumar and Hari Deo Sharma, *Selected Works of Motilal Nehru*, volume VI, Delhi: Nehru Memorial Museum and Library and Vikas Publishing House, 1995, p. 13.
74 Ibid., pp. 156–57.
75 Ibid., p. 152.
76 Sumit Sarkar, 'Editor's Introduction', *Towards Freedom: Documents on the Movement for Independence in India—1946*, Part One, Indian Council of Historical Research and Oxford University Press, 2007, pp. xiii-xxix, pp. xxi-xxii.
77 Chintan Chandrachud, *The Cases That India Forgot*, Delhi: Juggernaut, 2019, pp. 25–48.
78 Shylashri Shankar, *Scaling Justice: India's Supreme Court, Anti-Terror Laws and Social Rights*, New Delhi: Oxford University Press, 2009, p. 127.
79 Ibid., p. 124.
80 Neera Chandhoke, 'The Chequered History of Social Rights in India', in *Reinventing Social Democratic Development: Insights from Indian and Scandinavian Comparisons*, edited by Olle Tornquist and John Harriss, with Neera Chandhoke and Fredrik Engelstad, Copenhagen: Nordic Institute of Asian Studies, 2016, p. 198.
81 Human Rights Law Network, *Right to Food*, 4th ed., Delhi: Socio-Legal Information Centre, 2009, p. 8.
82 Shankar, op. cit., p. 152.
83 Chandhoke, op. cit., 2016, pp. 199–200.
84 See Upendra Baxi, *The Crisis of the Indian Legal System*, New Delhi: Vikas, 1985; also, Madhav Khosla, 'Making social rights conditional: Lessons from India', *International Journal of Constitutional Law*, vol. 8, no. 4 (2010), pp. 739–65.
85 Gaurav Vivek Bhatnagar, '"Bloodbath": Activist Nikhil Dey on NREGA Budget', *The Wire*, 1 February 2023.
86 Asmi Sharma and Nancy Pathak, 'Narendra Modi's Decade in Power has Brought a Shrinking Welfare Landscape to India', *The Wire*, 27 September 2023.

87 Shreehari Paliath, 'Jean Dreze interview: The main purpose of central welfare schemes today is to promote Modi', *The Scroll*, 11 February 2023.

88 Yamini Aiyar, *Seminar*, Annual Number, January 2023, p. 29.

89 Neera Chandhoke, 'A Handful of Grain: Is That All Citizens are Owed?', *The Wire*, 16 March 2022.

90 *CAD*, Volume I, p. 57.

91 Ibid.

92 Ibid., p. 60.

93 *CAD*, Volume XI, p. 975.

94 *CAD*, Volume VII, p. 38.

95 James Kierstead, 'Grote's Athens: The Character of Democracy' in *Brill Companion to George Grote*, edited by Kyriakos N. Demetriou, Leiden: Brill, 2014, p. 189.

96 E.H. Carr, *What is History*?, the George Macaulay Trevelyan Lectures delivered in the University of Cambridge, January–March 1961, UK, Penguin Books, p. 32.

97 James Kierstead, op cit, pg 188

98 *CAD*, Volume XI, p. 978.

99 Edmund Morgan, *Inventing the People: The Rise of Popular Sovereignty in England and America*, New York: WW Norton and Company, 1988, pp. 49–50.